# Working
# the
# System

# Working
# the
# System

Francis Gilbert

First published in 2009 by

Short Books
3A Exmouth House
Pine Street
EC1R 0JH

10 9 8 7 6 5 4 3 2 1

A CIP catalogue record for this book is available from the British Library.

ISBN 978-1-906021-75-7

Printed in Great Britain by Clays, Suffolk

Cover and inside illustrations © foxillustration.com

For Suz – friend and survivor
In memory of Jan

# Contents

# Introduction

*Believe nothing merely because you have been told it.*
*Do not believe what your teacher tells you merely out of respect*
*for the teacher. But whatsoever, after due examination and*
*analysis, you find to be kind, conducive to the good, the benefit,*
*the welfare of all beings – that doctrine believe and cling to,*
*and take it as your guide.* **Buddha**

**My experiences as a teacher**
I've taught in all kinds of state schools over the past twenty years.
During that time I've seen pretty much all that it is possible to
see: I've taught in institutions that have been bottom, middle
and top of the school league tables; I've taught in the socially deprived inner city, in affluent suburbia and in more rural
areas; I've taught in boys' schools, in girls' schools, and in mixed
schools; I've taught poor kids, rich kids, stupid kids, clever
kids, nice kids and very nasty kids; I've seen the whole range of
abilities, dealing with pupils who struggle to speak a word of English and students who could be the Einsteins and Shakespeares
of the future. In my worst moments, I've experienced classes

that have rioted, I've had missiles thrown at me, had ripped cans left on my chair, death threats issued to me; I've broken up fights, and on a number of occasions been hit. In my best moments, I've helped children of all backgrounds achieve their potential; given them enough of a boost to get top marks, to make fantastic presentations, produce great pieces of coursework. I've worked with, argued with and supported the whole gamut of parents: violent parents, bullying parents, loving parents, mentally ill parents. I've held numerous positions of responsibility: I've worked in the field of English as an Additional Language, in Special Educational Needs, Careers' Advice, Personal, Social and Health policy, and been Head of Department. So I've done my time. I am still a practising teacher, working part-time in a large comprehensive in outer London and writing the rest of the time.

But the real reason why you should read this book, and why it is different from all the ones out there is that it is an insider's guide, one which tells the truth. My first book *I'm A Teacher, Get Me Out Of Here* was a bestseller because it blew the whistle on what goes on in many schools throughout the country. It laid bare in vivid detail the bad behaviour, the arcane bureaucracy and the managerial idiocy that was once commonplace in many state schools. In particular, it revealed the damage that a poor headteacher can wreak upon a school. In the first school I worked in, the Head was very weak: her expectations of the teachers and the pupils were low. She rarely ventured outside her office and didn't have any clear rules that she expected the pupils – or the teachers – to follow. As a result, sensing that no one in charge would censure or even notice them misbehaving, many pupils and teachers did exactly what they wanted. At that time, during the early 1990s, the first league tables were published: the school I was teaching in was bottom of all of them. Only 3% of pupils attained five A-C grades. In a year of a 120 pupils, this effectively meant barely two pupils got the minimum grades expected of them.

The school was every parents' nightmare: riotous behaviour, appalling results, disaffected teachers and a general atmosphere of drift and decay. Not surprisingly perhaps, despite the fact that quite a few professional city-types lived in the area, there wasn't a single middle-class pupil in the school: the majority of pupils had free school meals and lived in households where English was never spoken. Most of them really struggled to speak, read and write English – and this had a huge impact upon their exam results. As a result, the few students who were native English speakers got royal treatment: in an effort to keep them interested, I can remember designing coursework with them which was much more inspired than any assignments I've set in the more middle-class schools I've taught in. And those students, by and large, went on to do well. Several studies recently have shown that when children from middle class backgrounds have gone to so-called 'sink schools' they've invariably been high achievers. This is partly because they've usually got very supportive parents who are willing to give them extra help, and partly because they get special attention in a school very keen to keep them.

In recent years,that rough comp has been utterly transformed. Under a new headteacher, it has become one of the most improved schools in the country, attaining results that put some suburban comprehensives in affluent areas to shame. The Head has managed to do this by: recruiting good teachers, imposing proper discipline and finding courses that are best suited to motivate the pupils. Since 1997, he's been greatly assisted by the extra funds that the Labour government has poured into inner city schools: besides attracting better teachers, he's been able to provide proper resources for his classrooms and reduce class sizes. It's all paid off handsomely. When I visited there recently I felt that the behaviour was better than in most 'middle class' schools and the teaching certainly much more inspired. I'd have no qualms about sending my child there.

## The complex truth about schools today

Unfortunately, 'superheads' like the one who turned around my old school are a little thin on the ground. Good headteachers are hard to come by and so there are still far too many substandard schools. The public's confidence in schools is dwindling, evidence of which can be found in the increasing number of parents failing to get their children into their first choice secondary school. In 2007, 14 per cent of pupils failed to get into their first choice school but a year later this figure had risen by three per cent. In metropolitan areas like London, the figure is much higher, with a whopping 34% of pupils failing to get their first choice school. If you live in an urban area, competition for the good schools is very intense – and many parents are left very disgruntled.

One rejected parent sobbed openly at the reception of the high-achieving secondary school where I now teach: 'But it's not fair! You have to let her in!' The school secretary had to ask for her to be escorted off the premises. But she wasn't surprised by this outburst. Every year, she gets hundreds of calls from panic-stricken parents wanting to know why their child hasn't got into our over-subscribed comprehensive. Every year, she says the same thing: read the instructions in the admissions booklet very, very carefully. There's no way she can explain such a complex process over the phone. If she did, she'd never go home.

I teach in a very popular, co-educational comprehensive in outer London which gets some of the best results in the country. In common with many similar institutions, every year, over 400 applicants don't get the place they want. Much as we would like to take them all, we have only one place for every three children applying. Every year, it's the same old story: there are always hundreds of bitterly disappointed families.

An authoritative report from the London School of Economics published in March 2009 suggests that the whole system is in a state of chaos, with schools flagrantly flouting the rules –

asking parents for personal information including marital status, occupation and even children's hobbies – and parents themselves being bamboozled by the arcane bureaucracy involved.

As a parent, teacher and writer who has researched this subject for years, I can only concur with the LSE's report. The central problem is that there is no consistency in the system: the rules or 'admissions criteria' by which schools admit their pupils differ from school to school. There are a host of different rules when applying to grammar schools, academies, faith schools, specialist schools and plain-old bog standard comprehensives.

If you're applying to a faith school, you usually have to prove you've attended church regularly for a number of years, live within the parish and have a glowing reference from your local vicar or priest. If you're going for a specialist school, you'll get preferential treatment if you can prove your child has an 'aptitude' in that specialism. For example, schools that specialise in sports will often need to see references from coaches and team leaders. For grammar schools, you'll need to pay for a private tutor so that your child will excel in the 11-plus exam. And if you're going for a good local comp, you might have to consider selling your house and moving closer to the school – or lying about your address. Later on in the book, I explain these rules more fully, but they are complex, and getting to grips with them takes time and patience.

Even moving near a good school can backfire. One parent I know moved to be near the only popular school in her area, a faith-based school that specialised in languages. She thought she had everything covered – attendance at church, the vicar's references, the proof that her son has an aptitude for languages – only to find that in the year of her application her Local Authority had switched to a lottery system: all the schools were allocated randomly. As a result, her application failed. She was faced with the absurd prospect of having to drive her son miles away to a sink school, despite the fact that she now lived next to an excellent one. All her hard work was in vain. 'This Government has ruined my family's life,' she told me, trying to hold back the tears.

But it isn't only the school admissions system that the Government has broken. It's the exam system as well. Since they arrived in 1997, Labour apparatchiks have done nothing but interfere with exams. Each new initiative has made things worse. The SATs exams for seven, 11 and 14-year-olds have been mired in controversy from the start, with claims from parents and teachers that they are irrelevant and put pupils under unnecessary pressure. The situation was so bad in 2008, when swathes of SATs papers were lost and thousands denied their results, that the Children's Secretary, Ed Balls, decided to abandon SATs for 14-year-olds and indicated that he was even considering scrapping the exam for all ages – a ghastly admission of defeat.

Even more seriously, A-levels and GCSEs have lost their credibility. The Government trumpets that the number of pupils gaining five A*-C grades at GCSE has risen from 44 per cent to 65 per cent since 1995, but any teacher knows this supposed improvement is nonsense. Recent research by Durham and Cambridge universities shows that the exams have become so dumbed down that these statistics are meaningless and that far from fostering real learning, the exam system has made our children less intelligent than they were in the 1970s, when far less public money was being spent on education.

Meanwhile, the world education rankings run by the respected Organisation for Economic Co-operation and Development (OECD) – the only really trustworthy league table there is – shows Britain slipping from fourth to 14th place for reading and from eighth to 24th for Maths. Put simply, most children from Europe and the Far East outperform our pupils every time – even in English.

Our exam system has become such a joke that many schools are giving up on it. One of our top independent schools, Manchester Grammar, decided to abandon GCSEs, on the grounds that they were too easy, and to replace them with the International GCSE (IGCSE). In a letter to parents, the Head poured scorn on the new GCSEs that the Government is introducing this September, observing that they threaten teachers' abilities to do their jobs well: they are stuffed full of easy questions and coursework.

Quite why the Government is introducing more coursework when its own investigations have uncovered widespread cheating and plagiarism appears a mystery, until you realise that coursework significantly boosts results. In other words, the revamp of GCSEs is a cynical ploy to manipulate the statistics. But as any experienced teacher knows, coursework has a corrupting effect upon pupils because it makes them believe they can cheat their way to the top.

One of the consequences of the Government's decimation of our exam system is that the process by which students apply for university has become farcical. The fact of the matter is that our best universities have lost faith in GCSEs and A-levels and have introduced their own tests. As a result, A-level students have to fill in a barrage of forms, write a personal statement and take exams set by the suspicious universities – particularly for popular courses such as medicine – before gaining a place.

To make matters worse, the university admissions procedure is so haphazard that there is no uniformity over when the universities make their offers. So students are required to accept or reject an offer before they've heard back from all the places to which they have applied. Having been tested to the point of extinction, these poor students are frequently forced to sign up for inferior courses, even though they may have gained places on better ones. As with school admissions, one suspects this is a cynical ploy to make sure that the inferior universities are filled with students.

Our education system is failing on too many counts: it is shockingly unfair, riddled with incompetence and corruption, and seems to benefit no one but the bureaucrats. While the pen-pushers enjoy enormous power and over-inflated wages, parents can see no end to their misery.

Put like this, it seems that there's no hope; that whatever a concerned parent does, their child will be poorly educated. As we have seen, one in five pupils won't get the school of their choice, every pupil will take exams which are devalued and dumbed-down, and too many students will go to sub-standard universities where they will saddle themselves with crippling debts to gain degrees that lead nowhere.

This is the reality for many parents who are not in the 'know'. The aim of this book is to help parents spot these problems when they arise and circumnavigate them. The truth is that if a parent knows the score, he or she can work the system to their own advantage and actually gain a damn good education for their child. But to do this, you also have to know the pitfalls. You have to be aware that many schools, teachers and qualifications are not fit for purpose. Once your eyes are open, you'll be powerful. Once you know about the schools to avoid and the teachers to complain about, you'll be able to ensure your child learns something. Once you know about the qualifications your child shouldn't pursue, you'll be able to make sure he or she takes the GCSE and A Levels which he needs to get into the best universities. Once you know how to deal with the many problems that will inevitably occur, you'll be in good shape to make sure your child gets the education he or she deserves.

For, interestingly, amidst the chaos the government has created with its blizzard of initiatives, it has also introduced legislation which gives parents much more power than they used to have, and, as a consequence, has made schools more accountable than they used to be. This book will show you how to use that legislation to your advantage.

The fact of the matter is the Labour Party has made it imperative that every parent wises up and learns how to work the system... In the past three years, practically everything has changed – and it is not all bad news.

## An outline of the book

My book is structured so that it blends personal stories and case histories with practical advice. My chapter on 'Good Attitudes' includes some important points about the ways children learn and some crucial advice about how you can support your child and enable him or her to do his best at school. After this, in the section on 'Admissions', I deal with the thorny issue of how to get your child into a good school. The procedures for this are very confusing and change constantly, but I take you through the essentials that will enable you to spot where the good schools are and do your best to get your child into them. Once in a good school, you and your child will be faced with a host of new challenges. My chapter on 'School Involvement' looks at all the major issues connected with getting involved with your child's school: how to help your child settle into school, what to expect from your child's new school and becoming a school governor. Related to this is my next chapter where I examine 'Learning', looking at what your child should be learning at school: the key guidelines here will help you work out whether your child is learning the right things. I then look at the vital area of your child's well-being in my chapter on 'Health'. This is followed by two linked chapters on 'Behaviour' and 'Bullying', which look at all the major worries parents have about schools: detentions, exclusions, solving bullying problems, sex and drugs.

I have included a large chapter on 'Special Needs' because this is an increasingly vital area in which parents need to be well informed. Here, I help parents diagnose possible learning difficulties their child might have, and give advice about how to treat them. My chapter on 'Assessment' explains in a clear fashion the complexities of how children are assessed in state schools, looking at Key Stage tests, GCSEs and A Levels and giving valuable tips about how your child might improve his performance in these crucial exams. Finally, my 'Conclusion' sums up the most important advice in the book.

The advice given here is applicable to any state school, whether it has a great reputation or a terrible one. There are good and bad teachers in every school in the country. What's great about state schools now is that there is a growing consensus, based on conclusive research, about what good teaching is. And there are now quite a few checks and balances in the system that enable parents to hold teachers to account if they are not up to the job: my book explains what these are and how you can use them to get the best education for your child.

# Good Attitudes

*If a child lives with approval, he learns to live with himself.* **Dorothy Law Nolte**

**What kind of childhood do you want your child to have?**
I have to confess my attitudes have changed. There was a time when I believed the best education I could give my child was academic. Perhaps that explains why my wife and I sent our son to a prestigious prep school from the age of four. We got what we paid for in his early years: by the end of his reception year, at the age of five – after extra coaching and some tearful sessions – he could read fluently. By the age of six, it was clear that he had all the basics in place.

But gradually it dawned me on me that something wasn't quite right. Both Erica and I were working flat-out, full-time, and employing a nanny to pick our son up from school. Although Blake wasn't desperately unhappy, I was concerned to hear that he wasn't really playing games during break-time and that he seemed burdened by all the homework.

Then something in me snapped. I had been running a big department at the school where I was teaching – but it was becoming too much with my writing and family commitments. Partly induced by the stress I was under, I slipped a disc and was in considerable pain for many months. This setback made me re-evaluate everything. I decided to give up my responsibilities at the school and become a part-time teacher, so that I could take over our nanny's role. I wanted to be more involved with my son's day-to-day life. He was now eight years old and growing up fast.

One morning, I had an epiphany: I remembered my grandfather talking about his childhood. How he used to play in the fields all day, roaming around the countryside in Northern Ireland with his brother, not being educated formally until he was nine years old. It didn't harm him in the least: he went on to become a lecturer in Mathematics at a top university, and was writing papers until the day he died, in his nineties.

That same morning, as I dropped Blake off at school and saw the faces of the anxious parents hastily kissing their children goodbye and rushing off to work, I thought: this is a really screwed-up world. Most middle-class parents nowadays would be horrified if their children spent all day unsupervised, 'learning nothing', in the fields, and yet what in the end was better? The 24-hour supervision that has become the norm in modern life or the unsupervised freedom that my grandfather enjoyed?

Was I robbing Blake of his childhood by sending him to this school? During the term, he barely had any time for himself. Every day, he would wake up and be shuttled early off to school, sitting for nearly an hour on the bus, then sitting through a day of intensive lessons, copying from the board, copying from text books, copying from pictures, filling in worksheets. Picked up at three thirty by our nanny, he took an hour to get home, where after tea, he spent an hour doing his homework, reading, writing, doing sums. After that came his music practice: the recorder and the guitar. By the time I came home from work at six thirty, he was ready for bed, knackered by everything he had to do.

The words of Tony Shepherd, a vicar I met in Harrogate, nagged at the back of my mind. He told me: 'I do think that parents can be overly enthusiastic about the wrong things. Parents are quite keen that there should be a lot of worthy homework for their children. When I make pastoral visits, I feel a little anxious about seeing parents towering over their small children, making them do their homework. A child has a solid working day and needs time to relax and be a child. There needs to be more sense of play and games. Ultimately, you make children enthusiastic about learning if you make them enthusiastic about life. My experience is that children don't do things like riding through woods on bikes any more and this is a great shame.'

By the time he was eight, Blake was doing OK at school. But I was beginning to notice that his progress was stalling and he simply wasn't as keen as he once had been. He is a bright boy, full of ideas, but the thought of writing didn't inspire him. Far from it. It seemed to fill him with dread. The work that came home was rigorously old-school: fill-in-the-gaps worksheets, punctuation and grammar exercises, basic arithmetic exercises. There were no wide ranging projects to do on the earth, the sky, the sea.

When I asked Blake about this, he told me that for most of the time he was expected to sit and work in silence, copying work off the board.

Copying is not a developmental activity: neurologically it engages only a small part of the brain. It discourages genuine original thought and fosters a real fear of new ideas. When I put this to Blake's teacher, he responded that copying was a useful way of getting handwriting practice. Here again he's wrong. Handwriting is far better practised in context, with children doing meaningful, purposeful exercises that actually require handwriting to be legible: writing letters, stories, reports, and posters.

Copying certainly gives the appearance of learning: the pupils' books are full of neat notes and comments, looking like they have absorbed a great deal. But scratch under the surface and you see they've learnt very little: just some basic information about how to punctuate and how to spell. While obviously these things are important, it is crucial that they are taught in context: that pupils write with a real purpose, that more often than not, they make up their own story rather than copying a page of *Harry Potter*, that they structure their *own* leaflet explaining why it rains rather than copying from a text book, that they create their own poems rather than copying one from an anthology.

The parents' evening when I discuss Blake's progress was a turning point for me. Overwhelmingly, I got the sense that the teachers at his prep school were stuck in the 1950s: they valued rote learning, comparisons between pupils, unnecessary competition, silent working, and lots of copying. It was at this point that I started to look at other schools.

The state primary schools that Erica and I saw covered the full spectrum: from the very bad to the brilliant. We re-visited a school which we'd initially rejected when Blake was four years old: at that time it was a failing school with a rotten Ofsted report and even worse results at Key Stage 2, with barely one in ten pupils gaining the expected levels in English and Maths when they were 11. This was partly because 98 per cent of the pupils were from ethnic backgrounds and didn't speak English as a first language, but it was also because they hadn't been well taught. Successive Ofsted reports had noted that there was a very high teacher turnover and lessons were very pedestrian, with far too much copying and colouring-in going on. For a few years the school had had no permanent headteacher, but now a new one was in post. She seemed energetic and full of ideas. I liked her a lot: she was clearly going to turn the school around. However, she was honest with me: much of the teaching was sub-standard and the class that Blake would go into if he joined the school was a particular problem. Although she wouldn't elaborate fully, it was clear that she was aiming to get rid of the teacher. On a tour of the school, we saw him teach: I could immediately see what she meant. He was an elderly Indian chap who mumbled in impenetrable English which even I couldn't comprehend. On the rest of our tour, I realised that the school, although very pleasant and affable, did not have much of a work ethic: most of the lessons I saw did indeed involve colouring-in and copying. The headteacher actually warned me not to send Blake there. 'I really need a year in post to turn this place around,' she said to me. I was grateful for her advice: I realised that I couldn't happily send Blake there. The school had many of the typical problems that the Labour government had inflicted upon schools: it had been blitzed with initiatives that hadn't worked. Standards had been neglected but resources hadn't: there were lots of great computers, interactive whiteboards and gleaming equipment in the school gym; but good, reliable, committed teachers seemed thin on the ground. I believed the new head would turn things around, but at that point, having been in the post only a few weeks, she hadn't made much of an impact.

The other local state primary we saw couldn't have been more different. It was bigger, had a much more stable staff and had gained better results. Like the other school, it was very well resourced, but these resources were clearly put to good use. The headteacher was a no-nonsense, old-fashioned teacher who made sure that the staff and pupils pulled their weight. We saw pupils working hard in every classroom: there was no copying and not much colouring-in. Most of the pupils were busy writing their own stories, solving their own maths problems, doing their own maths experiments. The class that Blake would join was working with a professional music group, learning about the different musical instruments. Above all, I saw the pupils 'actively' learning. They were obviously encouraged to discuss things with the teacher and their peers, both to work in groups and work independently, and to cover all the basics: reading, writing and arithmetic.

Even more interestingly, discipline at the school was superb. At his prep school, Blake had complained that he was too frightened to go out at break because the Headmaster had refused to ban hard balls, cricket bats and leather footballs. This had meant that most of the girls and many of the boys who were not that sporty stayed indoors during break-times for fear of being hit by flying balls and bats. The headteacher here had been faced with a similar dilemma but she'd banned hard balls and bats.

Contrary to the stereotype, the primary school did not ban competitive games but actively encouraged them. There were clubs that taught football, cricket, and basketball.

Reassured that the school was not a victim of the Labour Party's education policies, that it had managed to cherry-pick the best initiatives and retain good staff, I talked things through with Blake and my wife. We decided to apply to the school. Since there were spaces, we were successful: Blake started after half-term.

Since then, things have gone well. Above all, I've noticed the value of Blake feeling and being part of the local community. Having felt for so many years excluded from our local streets and parks, now we feel part of them. Instead of being trapped on a crowded bus before and after school worrying about his homework, he's larking around in the park. After school, he can play with his friends in the playground, laughing, jumping and running around in the way that children should.

His new school is not perfect, and I know it won't always be an easy ride, but the main thing is that now he is happier and more confident, finding learning fun and interactive, and enjoying making friends in his local community.

**Being a supportive parent**
Good teaching is, of course, very important if your child is going to achieve, but most research shows that it is good parenting which is the decisive factor in how well your child does at school.

The most significant and detailed research ever carried out into the influence of parents on their children's education was conducted by Charles Desforges in 2003 (http:// www.dcsf.gov.uk/research/data/uploadfiles/RR433.pdf).

In a summary of his findings, Desforges writes: 'Parental involvement takes many forms including good parenting in the home, including the provision of a secure and stable environment, intellectual stimulation, parent-child discussion, good models of constructive social and educational values and high aspirations relating to personal fulfilment and good citizenship; contact with schools to share information; participation in school events; participation in the work of the school; and participation in school governance.'

Translated into clear advice this means parents should:

**Be consistent.** Have consistent rules, routines, and attitudes. You should discuss some clear rules for your children to abide by. Crucially, they should be agreed between you and the child, but your child should be aware that you are ultimately the one who has the final word on what happens. This means discussing reasons for being positive in outlook, being polite, organised, punctual and hard working; having definite meal times and a proper bedtime.

**Stimulate your children.** As a parent you have a unique opportunity to turn everything from eating breakfast and doing household chores to going shopping at the supermarket into stimulating experiences by making them jolly and lively, full of genuine learning and love. Use books, TV, newspapers and trips to museums, theme parks, galleries, farms, relatives and friends to make your child's life interesting. Everything and anything is potentially magical: the sunshine, the taste of an apple, a lovely cuddle, a smile, a walk down the street.

**Discuss things.** Talk about your interests, your job, your feelings, your thoughts, your fears, your anxieties, and your positive and negative sides. Be as honest as you can! And listen to children in return. Remember a discussion is a two-way process: you are not lecturing; you are listening and responding to what your child says. Be encouraging and give praise where you can.

**Be positive and open-minded about learning.** Appreciate that potentially anything and everything is a learning experience and that mistakes are often the best way to learn about something. Talk about what society values as 'learning', what the school values as learning, what you value as learning. Talk about what your child does at break-time, their friends, their fears, their ambitions.

**Aim high.** Have high aspirations for your child and high expectations about how they will do in society. Encourage them to think that they can offer a great deal to the world around them. Have high expectations of what they will accomplish at school but don't feel that they must achieve highly to gain your love. Make it clear your love for them is unconditional. So you might say, 'I know you can get top marks in most of your subjects. We just have to figure out a way that you are going to do that. It doesn't matter whether you fail, but you need to give it a go. I'll always love you no matter how you do, but equally I know you can do very well with your work.'

**Get involved.** This means going along to parents' evenings, concerts, sports' days, coffee mornings, turning up at the school gates, looking at all the notice boards, asking questions, helping out at the PTA. If you feel so inclined you could become a parent governor or join a parent council.

### How the Harry Potter books can help you become a better parent

Psychologists generally agree that are three main types of parent: the autocratic, the permissive, and the democratic. Fascinatingly, J K Rowling's novels illustrate these types of parent and show the pitfalls involved.

**The Autocratic Parent.** This type of parent rules the house with a rod of iron, giving their children rules and regulations left, right and centre. They can be most commonly heard exclaiming, 'You can't do that!', and frequently requiring their children to obey arbitrary commands. If a child shows the slightest inclination to question orders then there is hell to pay: different points of view are not tolerated and perceived as insubordination. These parents are likely to be 'pushy' parents as well: making their children do activities which they may not enjoy but which make them look good in the eyes of the world. They will hire private tutors to make their child pass the exams to get into a grammar school and will demand to know why their child isn't given more homework – even when the child is very young. Autocratic parents are socially aspiring, viewing education not as an end in itself, but as a means of social advancement for their child. Autocratic Parents tend to produce children who are unable to express their feelings or even know what their feelings are; their children are distant, rarely hugging or touching them. On the surface, their children may be very successful but there will often be a well-spring of anxiety beneath the surface. They are terrified of failure and will work extremely hard to avoid it; they are motivated by fear of failure and do not enjoy the process of learning; it is merely a means to an end. Above all, they strive to be 'perfect', perceiving that there is a clear right and wrong way to do things, and that true success is measured by the results achieved at the end. Very good fictional examples of Autocratic Parents are the Dursleys in the *Harry Potter* books. Vernon Dursley and his wife Petunia are Harry Potter's adopted parents throughout the series and try to crush the magic out of their adopted son by imposing all sorts of arbitrary and unreasonable rules and restrictions upon him, keeping the truth about Harry's real parents from him for many years.

**The Permissive Parent.** At first glance, the Permissive Parent is the opposite of the Autocratic one. Where the Autocrat has rules and regulations, the Permissive Parent has none; where the Autocrat tightly controls what their children do – who they see, when and where they go out, what they do – the Permissive Parent, under the guise of being 'nice', lets their child do whatever they want. There are no set meal-times, bedtimes, or firm boundaries about what behaviour is unacceptable. The Permissive Parent is a lazy parent, preferring to offer bribes in order to get what they want from their child rather than paying them serious attention. However, this kind of parent may well think they are tremendously supportive towards their children, lavishing them with unearned praise. The Permissive Parent sees their child as their closest friend and confidante, frequently using their child as a sounding board for their problems, a moral crutch. These parents are likely to produce children who are not used to being given any boundaries or thinking about them, who frequently act before thinking, quickly becoming angry if their desires are not gratified immediately or overly emotional when they are thwarted. Moreover, their children have learnt to distrust much of what their parent says, treating their hollow praise with the contempt that it deserves. These children, cocooned in a world of false approbation and instant gratification, are complacent but also full of self-doubt behind their smug façade. They hate making mistakes and would rather not do an activity than fail. They expect immediate success. Often they lack the organisational skills and mental stamina to embark upon a prolonged period of study. Once again, the example of the Dursleys, the adoptive parents of Harry Potter, is instructive here; they treat their real son, Dudley, over-indulgently, allowing him to do whatever he wants. As a result, he grows up fat, unimaginative and unhappy, unable to cope with the vicissitudes of life.

**The Democratic Parent.** This parent is the model all parents should aim for; a parent who discusses things with their children, setting clearly explained and reasonable boundaries and having high but not unrealistic expectations of their child. Above all, the Democratic Parent believes in the power of language to resolve issues. Rather than seeking to bury possible problems with silence or arbitrary orders like the Autocratic Parent, or ignoring them completely like the Permissive Parent, the Democratic Parent listens to their child, helping them articulate their thoughts and feelings about a predicament. This kind of parent is not pushy but will encourage their child to give new ideas and ventures a good old college try. However, if it is clear after a few goes that their child hates their ballet lessons after school, the Democratic Parent will not force them to carry on. Democratic Parents are honest: they will own up to their mistakes and discuss how they intend to get over them. Their children are, on the whole, secure, confident and happy, and able to articulate how they are feeling. They do activities that they enjoy and take pleasure in the process of learning; while attaining good results is important to them, they have a sense of perspective and are not overly anxious about failure. They view making mistakes in a positive light, seeing them as an opportunity to do better next time. Again, the *Harry Potter* books offer a possible version of Democratic Parents in the portrayal of the ancient wizarding family of the Weasleys; the family is a happy one, despite the chaos caused by seven children and the evil machinations of Lord Voldemort, because discussion is at the heart of all they do.

The reality of the situation is that most parents exhibit signs of being autocratic, permissive and democratic while they are bringing up their children; we all have our moments of exasperation when we shout out arbitrary rules or bribe our children to behave.

However, it is the model that predominates which is the important one: if we bear in mind that it is the democratic approach which works best then this can help guide us to be better parents.

### The importance of praise

'Oi, you little c\*\*t, why can't you hurry up you slow coach?' I heard a mother say this to her son recently outside a swimming pool changing rooms. An eight-year-old boy was doing his best to stuff his wet towel into his bag but it wasn't fast enough. A little later, he started banging a vending machine violently, demanding a chocolate bar. Hearing the great thuds, his mother pleaded, 'Look, I'll get you a chocolate bar. I'll get you one, just f\*\*king stop that racket.'

I reflected upon the mixed signals that the mother was sending to her child: having been assailed for patiently putting away his kit, he was pacified from vandalising the vending machine with a bribe. Having taught a great many children with similar parents, I knew he'd be a difficult child to teach: a child who had learnt the implicit message that violence is generally rewarded with bribes, and good behaviour is usually ignored, or, quite frequently, punished. He'll probably have learnt a very similar message at school: well behaved children who quietly get on with the work are usually ignored or urged to work even harder, while badly behaved children get all manner of extra attention.

Is it any wonder that Britain's children are, according to an authoritative UNICEF (United Nations Children's Fund) report published in 2008, the unhappiest in Europe?[1] We live in a country where many parents, from all social classes, are uniquely ill-equipped to bring up well-balanced children.

At the root of the problem are the mixed signals that adults in Britain send their children. On the one hand, we monstrously sentimentalize children with our sickly sweet films and p resents, and on the other, we ignore children when they're being good.

As we have seen with Desforges' research, it is parents' influence which is the single most important factor in a child's success at school, no matter whether that is the top school in the land or the worst.

And furthermore, **it is parental praise which is the greatest motivation for a child**: not endless presents, trips to Disneyland, computer games or TV, but consistent, heartfelt and honest words of encouragement.

And this is a lesson I have to keep reminding myself of: it is a great deal easier to criticize my own child and my pupils than to praise them: bad behaviour is much more noticeable than good. But I now know that well-chosen words of praise which say precisely what I have liked about a pupils' work or behaviour are better at keeping good order than all the detentions in the world.

---

1   http://www.unicef.org.uk/publications/pdf/rc7_eng.pdf

## Turning nagging into encouragement

Praising well takes a bit of thought but often you can 're-shape' what might sound like nagging into positive words of encouragement.

| Common nags | Turning the nagging into encouragement | The psychology behind this |
|---|---|---|
| Why don't you ever tidy your room? | It would be great if you tidied your room by the end of the day | Making blanket remarks like 'you never tidy up', 'you're always rude', is very demotivating and defeatist. Saying that you would feel pleased if your child tidied his room and setting a clear deadline often works better. |
| Why do you always do badly in English? | You wrote a great story in English. | It's important to look carefully at areas where your child is not doing so well and praise precisely where they are going right. |
| You never read books. | I think you would really like this book. | All the research shows that more than rewards or prizes, personal recommendation of a book you have read is the decisive factor in getting your child to read. |
| Why can't you be quiet for once? | I'd feel much happier if you were quiet when I am talking to someone else. | Talking about your feelings and how your child affects them, instead of blaming your child, is more productive if you want them to behave. |

## The importance of reading for pleasure

One key factor in your child's future success in life is his or her attitude towards reading. Quite significant research completed by the Literacy Trust shows that 'parents and the home environment are essential to the early teaching of reading and the fostering of a love of reading. 84% of over 8000 pupils in a survey for Reading Connects indicated that it had been their mother who had 'taught them to read'. Research has also repeatedly shown that parental involvement in their child's literacy practices is a more powerful force than other family background variables, such as social class, family size and level of parental education.'[2]

It appears that when parents read to their children or recommend books to read, the impact upon a child's learning and well-being is astonishing. Just reading as little as five minutes a day to your child can significantly improve their attainment at school.

The best book for detailed parental advice on reading is *The Reading Bug* by Paul Jennings (Penguin, 2004).

## Why is it a good idea for my child to write a diary?

*'Always be nice to those younger than you, because they are the ones who will be writing about you.'* Cyril Connolly

One of the best ways to develop your child's writing, their analytical skills, their ability to reflect upon their achievements and improve their well-being is to get them into the routine of writing a diary. When they are very young you could encourage them to draw pictures, thinking about what has happened to them. The older they get, the more they can write. Encouraging them to write about:

---

2   http://www.literacytrust.org.uk/research/Reading%20for%20pleasure%20-%20summary.pdf

What has happened to him/her
What they have liked doing recently
What they have not liked doing
Their feelings
The reasons behind things/events

My son's writing has really developed as a result of keeping a diary: his ability to describe, explain, reflect, analyse and review. A lot of research suggests that writing a diary is deeply therapeutic; that people actually feel better after writing them, particularly if they've been anxious. Writing one yourself is a good way of encouraging your child. You could both write it at the same time.

## The importance of sport

Study after study has shown that encouraging your child to play sport is hugely beneficial: it encourages them to be healthy and fit, it boosts intelligence, and improves their ability to socialise. If he or she has an aptitude in a sport, it may help your child get into a school which specialises in sport.

**Do:**
Play sports with your child.

Encourage your child to do a whole variety of activities: dance, football, gymnastics, track events, swimming. Don't get them to specialise fanatically in a sport UNTIL they are 13 or 14. Research shows that the best athletes and sportspeople have had a rounded education in all sports before specialising.

Go swimming. Swimming is being cut back in schools and yet it is one of the most important physical activities your child can do. Try and make sure that your school offers a decent set of swimming lessons.

Talk it through. Remember the subject has an academic side as well: talking and discussing the science of movement and sports is very interesting and also very beneficial for PE.

**Don't:**
Order them to play a sport they hate.

Stand on the touchline criticising them.


## The importance of music

Encouraging your child to play an instrument or to sing can really help them in a host of ways. It greatly assists with improving their ability to appreciate and enjoy the world around them; some studies have shown that it appears to improve their intelligence[3] and it can help with reading in certain circumstances. It also seems to help children stay healthier and happier.

A Head of Music at a top comprehensive in the north of England gave the following advice for parents if they want their children to be good musicians.

**Do:**
Encourage your child to play an instrument early on: get them to play the recorder when they are six or seven.
Being able to play a musical instrument greatly assists with improving your child's academic attainment: there is a very strong correlation between high achievement in exams and musical proficiency.

Encourage them to practise a musical instrument regularly.

Get them to play and sing with groups of people, sing along with them. Get your child to see that music is a communal social activity. A school which is really serious about music will give your child the chance to sing in a

---

3   http://www.childcareaware.org/en/subscriptions/dailyparent/volume.php?id=46

choir or play in an orchestra.

**Don't:**

Force them to practise for hours on end.

Put unnecessary pressure upon them to pass music exams.

# Admissions

*There are no good schools, only good teachers.*

## The Secret Art of School Hunting

When hunting for schools, it's important to have a long-term perspective. Don't obsess over tiny details, instead try and think of the big picture. Think about where your child will be at the end of the process. Ultimately, it is your child's dreams and ambitions that should be considered.

## How do you hunt down a good school?

I am walking down the corridors of Sir John Cass secondary school in Tower Hamlets and it feels very weird. I am not dodging missiles, hearing abuse or witnessing scraps between children. This seems a totally different school to the one I taught at during the early 1990s; there isn't a fight in sight, not a shred of litter and the school now gets some of the best results in the country, instead of the worst.

Since Sir John Cass is near where we live, in east London,

we are thinking about sending our son here in a few years' time when he is old enough. Its recent Ofsted report rated the school as 'outstanding' and it is considered to be one of the most improved schools in the country. So here we are at the annual open morning, listening to the headteacher, Haydn Evans, as he guides parents around the site, describing the school's 'faith-based' ethos and firm discipline.

Everything we see in the classrooms confirms this. As we are walking, looking at the gleaming new facilities, a smart-suited parent tells me that a lot of his friends have moved to the countryside in search of good schools, but now he realises that they wasted their time. 'This school seems far better than any of the ropey old comps in the suburbs!' he chortles.

Many of the parents are anxious, asking questions about the school's results, how it deals with bullying, its extra-curricular classes. I am very familiar with their concerns because as a teacher I have fielded similar questions on numerous occasions during open days at other schools I have taught at.

At the comprehensive where I teach English, I have seen parents stalking around, clutching their bewildered children, notebooks in hand. Their eyes scan every gleaming piece of display work, every book they can lay their hands on, every computer, every Bunsen burner.

One parent confessed to me: 'As the girls are 11, I'm bracing myself, ready to face the nightmare zone. What school? This was a nightmare, I feel hysterical. My natural train of thought leads me from 'I chose the wrong school' to 'the girls are unhappy', to 'they will do badly in school' to 'they'll leave at 16 with no qualifications' to the inevitable conclusion that they will lead a life of deprived misery on the dole drinking homebrew surrounded by a brood of filthy children who don't know what melon is. This may seem ridiculous but the pressure of this enormous decision can be too much and you can go a bit mental. It's a bit like when you do badly in an exam and you think that the world has caved in and that the gate to your preferred path in life is well and truly bolted.'

During the 'open day' season for year 5 and 6 parents many parents seem bamboozled. Most boroughs will hold evenings at primary schools explaining the complex processes involved, but many parents remain confused. Few understand properly the admissions rules for secondary schools, and fewer know how to spot a good school, preferring to rely on myths rather than facts.

### How do you save time but also research schools properly?

Before schlepping around lots of schools, it is worth spending a few minutes on the internet. Log on to http://schoolsfinder. direct.gov.uk and, simply by typing in your postcode, you can see which your local schools are.

Your Local Authority (LA) will also provide you with detailed information about the schools in your area as well as vital information about how to apply for your chosen schools. You can either phone them direct or simply Google your LA's name and you should find their website very quickly, where all their relevant pamphlets will be ready to download as well. Read their information very carefully.

### What's all this about admissions criteria?

It is worth checking out the 'admissions criteria' of your local schools and any other schools you are interested in before long. This is the set of rules which your child will have to comply with if they are going to get into the school.

From September 2008, a new School Admissions Code has been put into practice. This is aimed at making the whole system fairer and clearer for all children and parents. The new code aims to:

• Stop schools discriminating against children from specific social and racial groups, or against children with disabilities or Special Educational Needs (SEN). Indeed, there is now 'positive discrimination' for SEN children.

• Stop schools asking about parents' backgrounds.

• Stop schools from seeing whether the parents had ranked the school first in their list of choices.

• Stop all hidden selection techniques such as demanding that parents give 'gifts' to the school or pay for expensive uniforms or text books.

• Allow schools to select 10% of their intake by 'aptitude' in their schools' specialism. So, for example, if the school has an official specialism in 'music', it may select 10% of its pupils who show 'aptitude' in music. [The meaning of 'aptitude' is interesting because it does not necessarily mean that the child is a gifted musician, it could mean that the child shows exceptional 'promise'.]

• Allows schools to admit siblings of pupils already at the school.

The bottom line is this: unless a school is 'faith-based', 'an Academy' or a 'grammar school', then the majority of its intake will either be siblings of pupils already at the school or drawn from the local area. Many schools do not have 'catchment' areas now but simply choose pupils who are nearest to the school – that is, if they are over-subscribed they take the children *closest* to the school. In urban areas, as a general rule of thumb, popular schools rarely take pupils more than 600 feet away from the school.

Some Local Authorities, though, are adopting school lotteries where all the pupils, within an area specified by the LA, are put into a lottery and their schools are allocated randomly. The LAs are justifying this to stop the so-called post-code lottery whereby affluent parents move next to the best schools and thereby stop poor families having a chance of getting a place there. The government is having second thoughts about the lottery system and may be curtailing it, but at the time of writing it is becoming increasingly popular with the zealous bureaucrats in the LAs. To me, it seems a great shame because it may destroy many good local schools since the lottery may mean that pupils from miles away go to them and local pupils are obliged to commute for hours to their allocated school. Education is too important to be decided by the spin of a wheel.

TIME SAVING TIP: In order to find out whether your child will get into a local school, phone up your LA and find out how far away the furthest pupil was in last year's intake. This will give you a good idea whether your child will make the cut the following year.

**Do:**
Check and see what the admissions criteria of your favoured schools are.

Read all the necessary information on your Local Authority's website.

Contact your LA if you are confused. Most have paid advisors to help explain things to you.

**Don't:**
Get into a panic: sometimes things are out of your hands and there is nothing you can do.

**How do you use Ofsted reports properly?**
Once you've drawn up a hit list of likely schools, it is then worth scanning through the most recent Ofsted reports for the schools. You can easily do this by logging onto http://www.ofsted.gov.

uk/oxcare providers/list, typing in your postcode and seeing your local schools come up. Do not bother with Ofsted reports which are more than three years old: they will be out of date and virtually worthless. Schools can change a great deal in three years!

The Ofsted reports often give precious information about whether a school really makes a difference to a pupil's attainment. In particular, the Ofsted report will give a clear picture of the standards of teaching and learning in the school overall, rating it from 1-4, with 1 being outstanding, 2 being good, 3 being satisfactory and 4 being unsatisfactory. Any recent Ofsted report that rates the standards of teaching and learning as 'satisfactory' or below indicates that the school is a bit mediocre. Similarly, the Ofsted report will give a ranking from 1 to 4 on the school's overall effectiveness, the behaviour of the pupils and a host of other areas.

In particular, look at the targets the school has set itself. These will give you a good idea about what to look for when you visit the school. For example, in a school near me, Ofsted set a target of 'improving the attainment of the Gifted and Talented students' in the school, indicating that the school was not stretching its most able pupils, but doing very well with students at the bottom end. Any parent of a high-achieving child would need to ask about this at an open evening.

**What are the top five things to look for in an Ofsted report?**

1 Its overall judgement on the school, its overall grading, the school's strengths and weaknesses.

2 Its judgement on the teaching and learning in the school.

3 Its rating on the behaviour of the pupils.

4 Its thoughts on the extra curricular activities for pupils.

5 Its thoughts on the well-being of pupils.

**League tables: which bits are important?**
Log onto http://www.dcsf.gov.uk/performancetables/ but read with caution! Don't trust the school league tables fully. The scrapping of the Key Stage 3 tests will mean that the league tables change a little, but it is unlikely that they will be ditched.

To use the league tables properly you will need to look behind the headline figures. In particular, check the maths and English scores at GCSE. If the school is getting below 50% A\*-C grades in these subjects, it means that more than half the pupils are not leaving school with the required minimum standards. This may not be a problem in a school where the majority of children have English as an additional language, but if that is not the case, be wary. Look also at the numbers of children gaining five 'good' GCSEs: in English, maths, the sciences, and modern foreign languages (MFL). Some schools may not offer much in the way of languages or sciences at GCSE. They should. At Sir John Cass, all the top achieving students are given the chance to study 'triple' science – physics, chemistry and biology (as opposed to the 'dual award' which mashes the three together) – and a host of languages.

**What do value-added scores mean?**
Does the school add 'value' to the pupils? In other words, does it make them learner faster and better? Schools that score below 100 on the league table could present a problem because it might be that they not stretching their students; the figures could show that they are merely trotting along at their expected levels or below, and are not achieving over and above what they have been targeted to achieve.

However, while you should consider the value-added scores, you should also be aware of the pitfalls involved in this. The notion of a school 'adding value' is very controversial. Since the early 1990s, the government has run 'Key Stage' tests for seven,

11 and 14-year-olds which have enabled statisticians to measure the progress that pupils make between each test. The statisticians then look at a child's GCSE and A-level results and compare them with the results they got when he or she was younger. From these measurements they can see how much 'value' a school adds to a pupil; pupils are expected to go up two levels between each test. If a pupil goes up *more than* two levels then the school is said to have added 'value' to the pupil. **Large scale analysis of these 'value-added' results have shown that many of the comprehensives that were judged to be the best schools are in fact failing to add value to the majority of their pupils.** For example, the school where I currently teach attains some of the best results in the country, but its 'value-added' score is quite low. This is not because it's a bad school – far from it! It's actually because it refused to offer the easier GCSEs and vocational qualifications that many schools offer in order to boost their value-added scores. Many schools, particularly in poorer areas, have boosted their value-added scores by insisting their pupils take 'applied' GCSEs in subjects like Information Technology; these GCSEs are stuffed full of coursework and count for statistical purposes as two GCSEs. They are, if truth be told, soft options. Many of the top universities now don't recognize them as serious qualifications.

In other words, the value-added scores should be taken with a pinch of salt. You'll need to check to see if the school is getting good scores through pushing 'applied' GCSEs. If they are, then you need to ask yourself whether you want your child to go to such a school, particularly if it means that the school doesn't offer 'gold standard' qualifications in subjects such as Modern Foreign Languages.

That said, the value-added scores *are* worth looking at because they do tell a story of sorts. If the scores are low and yet the school looks good, you should ask the headteacher why they are low. If his explanation doesn't ring true, then be wary!

**Why is my Local Authority important?**
Logging onto: http://www.dcsf.gov.uk/localauthorities/index.
cfm?action=authority will enable you to find out more about
your Local Authority and find their website.

Local authorities (LAs) are the part of your local council
which has a duty to provide information about education in
your area and promote high standards in all education sectors.
Whether they do or not is a moot point, but the central thing
to understand is that they are the first port of call when looking for schools and one of the last ports of call when you are
really dissatisfied with your child's school. All LAs have Educational Development Plans (EDPs) which set out, in typical LA
jargon, how they are going to make all their local schools fabu-
lous. For many parents the guff that the Local Authorities churn
out can be a nightmare, particularly where there are a number
of failing schools in their area. In order to be seen that they
are doing something, the LA will invariably produce numerous documents – action plans, strategic plans, improvement
plans etc – and expect parents to understand them. Usually, these so-called plans are actually 'ass-covering' exercises
whereby the LA avoids the blame for anything that goes wrong.
In recent years in some LAs, private firms have been hired to turn
failing schools around; these firms are even worse than the LAs
at spewing out self-serving pamphlets about how wonderful they
are, when, on the ground, schools have seen little improvement.
It's important that parents are not blinded by their glossy brochures
and look at the nitty-gritty; what is happening in the classroom,
in the assemblies, in the corridors, in the playground.

Ultimately, there is a real problem with accountability because nominally the LA is responsible for the education of every
child at a state school in their locale, but in reality, most LAs
have found great ways of shifting the blame for failing schools
onto other shoulders: headteachers, teachers, lack of resources,
lack of implementation of their ideas and so forth. You'll find it

very hard to pin the blame on the LA, but you must remember that when you've got a real problem, it's to the LA that you must turn for answers.

Most importantly for you, your Local Authority will have a prospectus booklet – commonly known as 'Information for Parents' booklet. It will include lots of important information: how to apply to schools with deadlines, the size of schools, how places are allocated and what happens if your preferred school has too few places for the number of applications.

It will also give you valuable information about what to do if you still don't understand the processes. More than 130 Local Authorities have Choice Advisors who will give you advice if you are confused. It is worth using them, but you must remember that they are employed by the LA or the government and may not give you impartial advice. It is overwhelmingly in their interest to make sure that all the schools are full, so that may mean that they advise you to send your child to a failing school, when that really isn't in the interests of your child.

For example, a Choice Advisor in my LA told me that the notorious failing school next door to me – which the police are regularly called to and is bottom of the league tables – was actually a very good school. They told me that parents who had initially appealed against sending their children to the school, but had been forced to accept it because it was the only one on offer, now felt it was a great place to send their child. This immediately made me suspicious: it turned out that the school was significantly under-subscribed and in dire need of more students in order to justify its existence. That said, the Choice Advisor was able to give me good advice about getting my child into the local oversubscribed school; he knew in considerable depth about the intricacies involved, including details of what to put on the admissions form when I applied. This is the great thing about these advisors: they know the various arcane procedures in the borough better than anyone. But often this information must be specifically requested, so make sure to come armed with questions, to get the most out of your advisor.

**Do:**
Use the Choice Advisors to advise you about how to get into a school.

Use them to help you appeal if you've been rejected from a school you particularly want your child to go to.

**Don't:**
Expect great advice about the best schools in the area.

### What type of school will best suit your child?
Increasingly, I have come to the conclusion that if you are in doubt, send your child to the school closest to home. There are huge advantages. Firstly, they are quickest to get to. The importance of this can't be over-estimated. The time that you gain by only having a short journey to and from school can be very productive: it's valuable time for catch-up lessons, music practice, socialising, having fun! If there is a problem with your child's progress, you actually have time to address it. The problem with sending your child to a school which is miles away with a good reputation is that the commute could be exhausting and counter-productive. Also, it will mean that all your child's friends are miles away too: you don't want to become a taxi service, ferrying your child backwards and forwards in the evenings and at weekends.

CASE STUDY **There are no good schools, only good teachers**
Caroline lived in an area in the South-east where there were a number of selective schools at secondary level: two grammar schools; two faith schools, which effectively creamed off the bright middle-class children who hadn't passed the 11-plus;

and a couple of comprehensives, which were basically sink schools stuffed full of children from dysfunctional and difficult families. She'd had a great time at primary school, learning the basics of the 3Rs, and achieving high Level 4s in her English and Maths SATs at 11, making her very slightly above the national average. To her dismay, all of her friends got into either the grammar schools or the faith schools, but because she wasn't tutored after school like all of her friends, she failed the 11-plus, and since her parents weren't religious or willing to lie that they were, she didn't get into the high-achieving faith schools. She went to the local comprehensive. She'd heard bad things about it, but nothing prepared her for what she encountered: riotous classes, endemic bullying, demoralised teachers, dispiriting lessons and an overwhelming atmosphere of drift and decay. She spent the first year at school trying to avoid being hit and punched: she was being bullied by some girls in the year above. Her parents' complaints fell on deaf ears. It wasn't until she came across an inspiring history teacher that things started to change for her. He was an exceptional and devoted teacher who had been in the school for a long time. Seeing that she was bright and willing to learn, he took her under his wing and would tutor her during lunch-times and after school. She quickly started surging ahead not just with her history but in all subjects: the extra confidence he brought made her bold enough to ask other teachers for extra work and guidance. They were only too willing to give it; Caroline soon found that she was receiving individual tuition in all the main subjects because of her pro-active approach. None of the other teachers were as good as her history teacher, but they made her aware of what she needed to know to get the top grades. Seeing that she was flourishing and gaining in confidence, a couple of her friends joined in with asking for extra work and guidance. As a result, Caroline attained As and A*s in her GCSEs, matching and in some cases exceeding the achievements of most of her peers at the grammar and faith schools. She went onto college for sixth form and studied for a history degree at London University, attaining a First. She now works in publishing and is thriving. She still says that her best teacher ever was that history teacher in her first year at secondary school. He had made all the difference.

Although it would be exaggerating to say that Caroline's history teacher turned her into a success, her story illustrates a crucial point: she did just as well, if not better than her peers at so-called 'good' schools because she found one good teacher who inspired her to take a pro-active approach to her learning. He enthused and motivated her in a way that many of her peers at better schools were not. Ultimately, what matters is not the good school your child goes to, but the teachers that your child gets at that school. Now there may be a higher probability that your child will get better teachers at a school which gets better results because 'good' schools attract better teachers. In my experience, this isn't necessarily the case. Some of the most high-achieving schools I've taught in have contained teachers who had tended to 'spoon-feed' the pupils to get the best results; in other words, the teaching itself has been rather pedestrian – there's lots of learning essay plans off-by-heart, lots of doing mundane exam preparation – because there's been an obsession with getting great results. Teachers in tough schools don't have the luxury of doing this: they'd have a riot on their hands if they insisted upon endless exam practice and learning from the text book. Instead, their lessons have to be interesting and inspiring to keep the pupils engaged. Moreover, I've noticed that far from the stereotype of the clever child being ignored by the teachers in a tough school, they're nurtured and looked after in a much more individual fashion than in a school which is stuffed to the rafters with clever kids.

As I mentioned above, recent research shows that children from more affluent backgrounds do well at state schools with average or below average results. Researchers from the Universities of Cambridge, Sunderland and the West of England (UWE) carried out 248 in-depth interviews with the parents and children who had made 'counter-intuitive school choices' in London, north and south England. Most children from the 124 families studied also did well at GCSE, with up to 15% going on to Oxbridge – way above average. The study said parents deliberately picked socially diverse schools, believing the experience would help their children become better, more 'rounded' people. They all encountered inspiring teaching along the way. Professor Gill Crozier of the University of Sunderland said: 'The children often get special attention as they are nurtured by teachers who are keen to give extra help to improve the school's results.'[4]

### When to listen to your child – and when not to

When choosing a secondary school, you must involve your child in the process. You need to ask your child what they think and discuss the options carefully with them. You need to find out what matters to them. I would, however, be against selecting a school just because the child's friends are going there. Or indeed not going there. I have spoken to several parents who have sent their child to schools precisely because their friends were going elsewhere, on the grounds that they wanted their children to make a 'fresh start'.

This is a very thorny issue – and may be the one that causes the most conflict in your household. The important thing to consider is: where will my child learn the most? If you know that your child's friends are distracting them a lot in class, getting them into trouble, then you may want to seriously consider finding another school for your child. However, you may find that similar problems occur in the new school; that your child is

---

4   http://news.bbc.co.uk/1/hi/education/7256628.stm

easily led, and simply finds new so-called 'friends' with whom to misbehave. In which case, all your efforts to send him or her to a different school, away from the bad influences have completely backfired. It's therefore worth your while investigating thoroughly why your child is being drawn into wayward behaviour. Discuss this with your child's teachers and see what they think. It may be that if the secondary school is forewarned about the bad influences they'll be able to put the offenders into different classes. It's my experience that children who go to schools where they know no one sometimes fall into behaving badly in order to prove themselves, and that attending a school where they know a few people can really help.

But whatever is the case, you mustn't be blackmailed by your child on this issue. Choose the school with the best teachers and atmosphere, not the most sociable one.


**The different types of school: choice or confusion?**
Many parents are confused by the number of different types of secondary school that exist: academies, city technology colleges, specialist schools, special schools, faith schools, local community schools, pupil referral units.

The differences between them may be many – and are outlined below – but the essential point is that they should all be judged on the same criteria: their academic record, particularly in English and maths; their most recent Ofsted report; the behaviour and attitude of the pupils; their extra-curricular provision and what you thought of them when you visited with your child.

The UN Charter of Human Rights recognises that all children have the right to be educated. In the UK, this means that all children are entitled to a free place at state school until they are 18. Most children start school at four or five years old, usually attending a primary school which they normally leave at 11, moving onto secondary school. It would be sensible to just have these two types of school, but unfortunately this isn't the case. Within these types, there are a number of different categories of school again. The categories of school change all the time, depending upon the whim of the government, so I have given the key ones here as simply as possible.

All of them are funded by Local Authorities (LAs). They are all obliged by law to follow the national curriculum and be inspected by Ofsted.

They are:

**Community schools**  are run by the Local Authority, which employsthe staff, owns all the land and buildings and decides the 'admissions criteria' – the rules by which children are admitted into the school. Usually these schools draw their pupils from the local community: their overwhelming emphasis is to generate an inclusive community atmosphere. At their best, they really reflect a diverse community, drawing from all classes and ethnic groups. At their worst, they can become sink schools because the middle classes in the area opt out of them.

**Foundation schools** are much more independent from local authority control than community schools because they are run by their own governing body, which employs the staff and sets the admissions criteria. Land and buildings are usually owned by the governing body or a charitable foundation. Within this category, there is now also a particular type of Foundation school, called a Trust School, which forms a charitable trust with an outside partner – for example, a business or educational charity – aiming to raise standards and explore new ways of working.

The decision to become a Trust school is taken by the governing body, with parents having a say. Trust schools will be introduced from summer 2007.[5]

http://www.trustandfoundationschools.org.uk

**Voluntary-aided schools** are mainly religious or 'faith' schools, although anyone can apply for a place. They are usually Church of England or Catholic schools. As with Foundation schools, the governing body employs the staff and sets the admissions criteria. School buildings and land are normally owned by a charitable foundation, often a religious organisation. The governing body contributes to building and maintenance costs.[6] Usually, two separate applications are necessary for Voluntary-aided schools: one to the school itself, and one to your Local Authority. (See below: '**How do you fill in the forms correctly?**') These types of school used to be quite independent of LA control and are sometimes accused of rigging the admissions process so that there is a long list of requirements, which basically favour middle-class children.

http://www.teachernet.gov.uk/management/resourcesfinanceandbuilding/FSP/voluntaryaidedschools

**Voluntary-controlled schools** are similar to Voluntary-aided schools, but are run by the Local Authority. As with Community schools, the Local Authority employs the school's staff and sets the admissions criteria. School land and buildings are normally owned by a charity, often a religious organisation, which also appoints some of the members of the governing body. These types of school are much less likely to rig the admissions process to favour middle-class children.

http://en.wikipedia.org/wiki/Voluntary_controlled_school

**Specialist schools** focus on a particular subject area. Examples include sports, technology or visual arts. There are over 2,000 specialist schools in the country. The government is aiming

---

5 & 6   http://www.direct.gov.uk/en/Parents/Schoolslearninganddevelopment/
ChoosingASchool/DG_4016312

to make all secondary schools 'specialist' in status. Bidding for specialist status takes up a huge amount of staff time, but brings extra funding. The problem with the whole idea is that you might not live next to a school which specialises in a subject your child likes. What do you do then? The current admissions code means you'll have to usually lump it. However, many specialist schools specialise in subjects like music and sports – both of which have a huge appeal. Encouraging your child to be sporty and musical is something you should do as a matter of course. You may find that there are lots of opportunities for your child to 'specialise' in these subjects in your local area: orchestras to join, music groups to participate in, football matches to play in and so forth. Encouraging your child to join in is no bad thing and may help them with attending the specialist school of your choice.

http://www.specialistschools.org.uk

**Academies** are independently managed, all-ability schools set up by sponsors from business, faith or voluntary groups in partnership with the Department for Children, Schools and Families and the Local Authority. Together they fund the land and buildings, with the government covering the running costs. Academies appear to be free of LA control and, as a consequence, enjoy more freedom when excluding children and dealing with children with special needs. They appear to be very well run but rather authoritarian places, often in the pocket of their sponsor. Personally, I like some of the things that they've done with the extra powers they have. For example, many Academies have an extended school day, frequently finishing at 4.15pm or 4.30pm, using the time from 3pm to allow children to do homework and independent study in school. This is a marvellous idea: children are able to use the resources of the school – the library, the computers, teacher expertise – to complete projects of their own. I think all secondary schools should do the same. Academies tend to be effective and more disciplinarian. Very popular with parents.

http://www.specialistschools.org.uk

**City Technology Colleges** are independently managed, non-fee-paying schools in urban areas for pupils of all abilities aged 11 to 18. They are geared towards science, technology and the world of work, offering a range of vocational qualifications as well as GCSEs and A levels.

http://www.standards.dfes.gov.uk/academies/ctcs

**Community and Foundation special schools** cater for children with specific special educational needs. These may include physical disabilities or learning difficulties. In the name of 'inclusion', the government has closed over a hundred of these schools since 1997.

http://www.specialneedsuk.org/parents/index.htm

**Faith schools** are mostly run in the same way as other state schools. However, their faith status may be reflected in their religious education curriculum, admissions criteria and staffing policies. Increasingly, Faith schools are tightening up their admissions criteria so that it's very difficult to get into them unless you have real proof of religious devotion: you'll need references from vicars, priests; proof you've attended church regularly for a number of years; evidence of living in the parish.

**Grammar schools** select all or most of their pupils based on academic ability. In total, there are 164 grammar schools, and it is likely that there are at least three secondary modern or 'community' schools for each grammar. The system affects about 1 in 10 pupils. Existing legislation makes petitioning and balloting to end selective admissions so impractical as to be virtually impossible. There will be no change to the system at a local level unless there is a new commitment to fairness at national level. In England in 2000, only 2.7% of grammar schools pupils were eligible for free school meals, compared to 17.1% in non selective schools, illustrating the social segregation caused by selection. In 2007, a DCSF-commissioned report confirmed that grammar schools have huge amounts of social segregation.[7]

http://www.ngsa.org.uk

**Maintained boarding schools** offer free tuition, but charge fees for board and lodging. Most schools are 11-18 schools, though there is one 13-18 school, two which offer Primary Boarding as well as Secondary Boarding and one 11-16 school with a nearby Sixth Form College.

http://www.sbsa.org.uk/index.htm

The bottom line is that all the different types of school, with their different types of criteria are very confusing. Does it mean more choice for parents? When all is said and done, no: it means far less choice because unless you meet the criteria, you won't get your child into the school.

You may well find that even though you live near many of these schools, you can't get your child into them because you're not religious enough, your child doesn't excel in a particular specialism, hasn't passed the 11-plus, doesn't live close enough to the school.

It's high time the government simplified the process: but until then, you'll have to live with it.

---

7  http://www.campaignforstateeducation.org.uk/Choice_or_Confusion_2008.pdf

**What do you look for when visiting schools?**
Before you get to the stage of visiting a school, it is worth noting that the government recently changed the law by which schools can admit students. Now, the majority of parents will have to choose from schools in their local catchment area. So it is most important to read the admissions criteria very carefully before you set your heart on a school.

Nearly all schools have open evenings and days when parents can have a good snoop around.

Some believe that open days can be misleading. 'Parents should make sure they go along during lessons and see how the teachers behave towards the pupils,' suggests Huda al Bander, 19, a veteran of London comprehensives and colleges. Al Bander is among a group of teenagers belonging to the Edge Learner Forum, a unique organisation working to promote practical learning in schools.

'A good school is a school where you will see teachers not only talking to the whole class but also working one-to-one with the pupils, listening to their questions and not putting them down.' 'And' she continues, 'good schools cater to pupils' different learning styles, and the best schools get the right balance between practical learning and theory.' Increasingly, educationalists are realising that pupils learn effectively in different ways and need chances to learn through dance, drama, art, music and doing presentations.

Equally, if you realise that your child is going to be sent to a school that you think is rubbish, you should try to keep your most negative opinions to yourself because they could affect your child's whole experience of the school. This is going to be increasingly important because 21% of parents don't get their first choice of school.

During the open evening, it is worth listening to the admissions part of the headteacher's speech and getting him or her, or someone else in the know, to explain it to you again if you don't understand it. This could save you an enormous amount of time and effort later: the last thing you want is to apply for a school at which your child can't possibly gain a place. Your open evening may be the last chance you have to talk to someone in the know about admissions criteria.

## What are the things to check out when you visit a school?

• Look at the work the children are doing. Is it challenging enough or is it too difficult? Is the work on display being marked carefully with helpful comments and targets at the end of the work? Are the pupils acting on the teachers' advice? If you've seen work which is produced at the beginning of the year – at the start of the exercise books – and you compare it with more recent work – at the end of the exercise books – can you see that there is a noticeable improvement? Is their writing becoming more detailed and complex?

• Is there good equipment? What are the computer and PE facilities like?

• Is it easy to get to?

• Are parents involved with the running of the school? Is there an active PTA which will give you guidance and help if you don't know how your child might get into the school?

## Killer questions for the open day

### Ask teachers:
Would you send your child to this school?

What would you do if I complained that my child was being bullied?

What evidence can you show me that my child will be stretched?

How does this school cater for children with learning difficulties?

What would you do if I complained about the quality of teaching?

What is good teaching?

(This last question is worth asking: remember that good teaching is about enthusiasm, high expectations, engaging all the students with interesting and valid tasks, assessing pupils' understanding and then setting work that builds upon what they already know.)

**Ask pupils:**
What level/grades are you achieving in English/maths/science?

What do you have to do to improve in these subjects?

What are the best things about lessons?

What are the worst?

How well behaved are the children?

What does the school do with bullies and disruptive pupils?

What are the dinners like and are the toilets kept nicely?


## Getting into a grammar school
Increasingly, grammar schools are the odd ones out in the state system. They are essentially a dying breed – even the Tories are considering disbanding them – but they remain popular with some parents.

Getting your child into an academically selective school is

time-consuming. The reality is that you will need to 'train up' your child so that he or she can pass the relevant exams. This involves preparation, planning at least two years ahead of the exam, assessing your child's abilities, buying past exam papers, coaching your child and being very patient.

The Grammar School Association estimates that 75,000 children annually sit the 11-plus for only 20,000 places. This means that the vast majority of children don't get into grammar school. And it really isn't the end of the world if they don't.

It is important to remember that all grammar schools are focused upon achieving the top results in the country, and they do this by rigorously testing their students at frequent intervals, and often weeding out the students who are going to achieve sub-standard results before they take public exams.

**Do:**

Consider a grammar school for your child if it is on offer. Visit it and judge it for yourself.

Remember there are alternatives.

Bear in mind that failing the 11-plus can be extremely traumatic. John Prescott, the Deputy Prime Minister, was still bitter about it over 50 years after he failed.

**Don't:**

Waste lots of money on extra tuition for passing the 11-plus. Your child's primary school should be teaching him or her properly!

Demotivate your child by piling on lots of pressure to pass the 11-plus. This can be very counter-productive in the long run.

For more information, log onto the home of the National Grammar Schools Association at http://www.ngsa.org.uk/index.htm

For free sample papers log onto: http://www.chuckra.co.uk/educational

## How do you look for good Sixth Forms?

Remember you have a great deal more choice about where to send your child when considering Sixth Forms. Sixth Form colleges, places of further education and schools with Sixth Forms essentially have the discretion to pick and choose pupils.

**Do:**

Talk to your child about what he wants to do in the future. Talk about everything, his dreams, his ambitions and his talents. Think about how he might attain his dreams. Draw up a plan.

Get some great careers advice. All state schools have careers advisors who will give their professional opinion about where might be best for your child. The government gives free careers advice at http://careersadvice.direct.gov.uk/helpandadvice/helpwithchildcare/ or by phoning 0800 100 900. Just as important and useful may be the advice you receive from friends, neighbours, relatives. Start cultivating every contact you know and ask for their help.

Draw up a hit list of possible places to go to by looking carefully at the Ofsted reports: look at Ofsted's overall judgement of the institution, its strengths and its weaknesses.

Visit your hit list. Ask the same questions you would if you were visiting a secondary school. Think hard about what kind of school you want your child to go to. Do they want to be in a school atmosphere with its system of form tutors and pastoral care? There is a big difference between Sixth Form at a secondary school and Sixth Form colleges. Sixth Form colleges and places of further education tend to be less about caring for the whole child and more about offering a wide variety of courses. They are more impersonal and anonymous, but some students, sick of the claustrophobic atmosphere of school, like that.

Talk to Sixth Form students. Ask them about the quality of the teaching and how much they are supported in the Sixth Form.

**Don't:**
Push your child to go to a school they don't like or to do subjects they don't want to do. At this age, it is very important they are motivated to learn.

## How do you fill in the forms correctly?

THIS IS VERY IMPORTANT! The number one rule is: if in doubt, check it out! Rules and regulations change all the time. See http://www.direct.gov.uk/en/Parents/Schoolslearnin ganddevelopment/ChoosingASchool/DG 10038421 for the most up-to-date information.

The form filling can be fiddly. The main thing is you must make sure you apply using your Local Authority's common application form. Some schools – Faith schools in particular – require that you send an application to them and one to the LA, while other schools require you to apply only through the LA. Again, checking this at an open evening saves much agony.

It is also worth finding out the best way to rank your schools on your form. Many LAs, including all those in London, operate a policy of offering one school place only, giving parents their highest ranked school that has places. This means that if a parent has put top of their list two schools for which their child does not meet the criteria, their child will not be offered a place at that school, but if they met enough of the criteria they would be offered a place at the third school.

Should you be given a third place, but you are not very happy about it, you can appeal to the first two schools. If you don't meet the criteria for any of the schools on your list, you will be given the nearest school to your house with spare places – often a very unpopular school which is miles away – so try to be realistic about your options and go for the best likely one.

The main thing to remember is that ultimately it is not the school that makes the real difference: it is you, the parents. Even if your child goes to a school you would never have chosen, given the right support at home he or she will succeed. However, if you do hunt down a good school and get your child into it, you'll be saving yourself much work and stress in the long run. If your child is not being properly taught, you'll need to fill in the gaps by either teaching them yourself or hiring private tutors.

TOP TIP: Many schools, particularly Faith schools, require that you apply both to the LA *and* to them.


**Can I do a Tony Blair and avoid sending my children to the local sink school?**

Before he became Prime Minister, Tony Blair famously and con-troversially sent his children to the London Oratory School, a successful, oversubscribed school in a posh part of Fulham, South-west London, rather than the school nearest to his then residence in Islington. It just so happened that he lived right next door to a notorious sink school which gained some of the worst results in the country and took in some of the poorest children in the borough. Blair benefited from the admissions code set up by the Tory government which gave schools like the Oratory much more freedom to pick and choose who they admitted. During his tenure as Prime Minister, the admissions code was tightened up to stop exactly the kind of jiggery-pokery Blair used when he wangled his way to getting his children in there. Parents now have to very strictly establish their commitment to the Catholic faith by handing in cast-iron proof of attendance at Sunday worship and so on; parents living in the local parish are also favoured.

The Oratory's admissions code is closely watched by the local Ombudsman so that it overwhelmingly favours the children of Catholics who live closest to the school. The code does not allow schools the latitude to admit the children of celebrity parents, no matter how powerful. So the long and short of it is this: you won't get your child into the Oratory if you live on the other side of London and don't have cast-iron proof of commitment to the Catholic faith.

Message to powerful parents hoping to twist the rules: the days of doing a Tony Blair are well and truly over.

## Working the system with specialist schools

While the kind of 'pushiness' that was exhibited by Blair won't succeed these days, there are still some ways of working the system. At the time of writing – though this may change soon – specialist schools can select up to 10% of their intake according to their first specialism. This means that parents who show that their children have 'aptitude' in the school's specialism – usually in sport, music, drama, maths, or science – get preferential treatment. Therefore, it's well worth your while looking at the specialist schools in your area and seeing if your child has an 'aptitude' in a particular specialism. If you have your heart set on a particular school, you should collect evidence that your child has an 'aptitude': attendance at coaching sessions, prizes, match reports are all significant here. Schools frequently ask for a reference from a specialist so you will need to think about a suitable person in that regard. They may also, in the case of drama places, ask for an 'audition'.

TOP TIP: Take advantage of all the extra tuition that Local Authorities now offer in sports and music. Many LAs offer extra coaching sessions in various sports and music schools for interested pupils. Log onto your LA's website to find out more.

## Was Paul McCartney right to send his children local state school?

The ex-Beatle is perhaps the most famous person to have insisted upon sending his children to state schools. It is alleged that Stella, his daughter, hated her time at state school in Sussex during the 1970s and 80s and was bullied, as well as becoming a bully herself. She has commented though that her time at the comprehensive school really toughened her up.

McCartney now wants his daughter by Heather Mills, Beatrice, to attend a state school as well. What seems to be most important for him is the social experience that state schools offer. Clearly, all of his children seemed to have benefited from an education which hasn't been rarefied: they've all achieved highly but seem not to have suffered from the addictions and mental problems that plague many rock star children. Their time at state school seems to have grounded them, given them a wider perspective and enabled them to flourish.

There's an important lesson to be learned from McCartney and that's not to be a snob or prejudiced about schools. I have spoken to too many parents who have consigned schools to the dustbin based on very flimsy evidence. They've condemned a school because they've seen a few kids misbehave outside school in school uniform, or one disaffected former pupil has warned them not to send their children there because it is full of chavs/Asians/whites/morons/drug-dealers. These sorts of blanket judgements are not helpful and usually totally untrue. Base your judgments on firmer ground than this.

Look at the most recent Ofsted and the surveys in them: they will be much more accurate than the hearsay of a few panicked parents and pupils. Look at the results for all types of children and the value the school adds to the pupils' results. Visit the school and talk to the headteacher, the staff, and the pupils. Look at the facilities on offer. Don't write off a school before you've even visited it.

Personally, I've found McCartney's attitude quite inspirational. Having experienced the difficulty of 'helicoptering' my child into a remote private school, I now appreciate just how great it is that he goes to a local school. He knows the children in his area. He goes out for a walk and says hello to the kids in his street. He plays with them in the playground next to us. And he has time to do other things. McCartney realised all of this was much more important for his children than mingling with closeted children from wealthy backgrounds.

**Do:**
Be open-minded about the local schools.

Realise the value there is in your child getting to know the children in his/her area if he goes to a local school.

Be positive about children no matter what background they come from. Don't write off entire schools because you've seen a few kids misbehave.

Remember all the statistics show that if you are supportive, your child will do well.

Remember that you as a family will gain valuable extra time if your child goes to a school near to your home.

**Don't:**
Panic. Worrying about what school your child will go to years ahead of time is pointless. The school may have changed a great deal in a few years.

Be a closet snob. Just because a particular ethnic group or social class dominates a school, don't feel your child can't go to the school because he/she isn't from it.

## How to spot good and bad headteachers

A few years back, I taught at a school that terrified me. Just walking down the corridor was hazardous. Frequently, children would rush up behind me and hit me on the back of the head, shouting out, 'Gilly, Gilly, how are ya doing, mate?'

When I complained to my head of year, he said I needed to get a sense of humour; he knew that there was nothing he could do about it. Chaos reigned in and out of class.

In one lesson, all the pupils pushed the furniture out of the classroom and lit cigarettes; in another, I was pelted with drawing pins. On one occasion I sat down on a chair which had been booby-trapped with ripped up cans, cutting my backside.

I didn't complain. It was pointless: I knew absolutely nothing would be done. My only option was to apply for other jobs, which I did – constantly. Unfortunately, I was considered a failure by potential employers for being at the school, and very few wanted me. The same applied to the majority of the staff, who were mostly desperate to leave but were trapped by the school's reputation.

A vicious circle had taken hold: poor, weak leadership had led to the school gaining very poor results, which had led to the demoralisation of the staff who couldn't leave, which led to even worse teaching. They were dark days. My long search for another job did eventually pay off, and I escaped to the leafier and more sedate suburbs of London.

As I mentioned in my introduction, I returned to the school recently and was astonished. Shortly after I left, the old head had been sacked and a new one put in place – a very different operator. My head had been a cultured, intellectual woman who had agonised, Hamlet-like, over the complexities of all the decisions she had to make. Her replacement was a simple, straight-forward, no-nonsense man, obsessed with imposing good discipline and getting the children to work hard. He walks around the school with a loudspeaker and fusses endlessly over the state of the pupils' uniform.

He and his management team check in on lessons all the time, yanking out miscreants if they step out of line. Even though the school has more or less the same intake – most of the children come from deprived homes – their behaviour couldn't be more different.

Instead of rioting, they line up quietly for lunch; instead of desperate teachers yelling for order, there is a studious hush in lessons; instead of books being flung around the head of a depressed librarian, silent working now goes on among the bookshelves.

The school exemplifies what Ofsted wants all schools to be. In its report, *Twelve Outstanding Secondary Schools Excelling Against The Odds*,[8] the schools inspectorate showcases schools in challenging circumstances that have been rated as 'outstanding' in at least two inspections and examines the elements that have created this success. Buried in the jargon is a very basic point: the best schools have great teachers who inspire their pupils; these adults assess their charges constantly and are always giving them feedback about how they can improve. Children flourish under this sort of treatment.

However, even the best teachers flounder when there is no law and order; which is where headteachers come in. A shocking majority – 66 per cent – of frontline teachers feels there is a discipline crisis in our schools and one of the reasons they cite is a weak headteacher. Great headteachers are old-fashioned creatures. Like Dixon of Dock Green, they patrol their patch religiously, learning the names of every pupil, making sure that the naughty kids are punished and the good ones are praised.

Worryingly, many hands-on headteachers are being replaced by glorified bureaucrats: sycophantic managerialists who are obsessed with implementing every Government initiative and

---

8  http://www.ofsted.gov.uk/Ofsted-home/Twelve-outstanding-secondary-schools-Excelling-against-the-odds

ingratiating themselves with the educational establishment. They spend too much time at conferences and rarely poke their heads out of their offices when they are at school. Instead, they issue diktats and set up complex reporting and monitoring structures in school that tie up the teachers in paperwork.

They are obsessed with data, putting facts and figures above people. They manipulate the curriculum to get good results: this might include encouraging pupils to take soft options, including syllabi stuffed with easy coursework assignments and implementing vocational courses that are impossible to fail. They deem teachers as no more than 'facilitators' of learning, libraries as 'resource centres', and failure as 'delayed success'. The name of the game is making sure that they are never blamed for anything and that they gain a great job after they leave their school – they rarely stay in charge of a school more than five years before moving on to the next sinecure.

### The best headteachers:
Support parents. They don't ignore parents' concerns and are very important allies if there is an issue that needs to be sorted out.

Attract, inspire and retain good teachers.

Impose good discipline: creating a culture which has clear, fair rules which everyone obeys.

Check that good teaching is going on, helping weak teachers to improve and good teachers to thrive.

Know all their pupils: they praise the good ones and punish the bad.

### The worst headteachers:
Demotivate their teachers and can't retain good staff.

Are unable to impose good discipline.

Rarely venture out of their offices.

## Key points when choosing a good secondary school for your child

**Do:**

Remember the advantages of choosing a local school: the proximity of the school will buy you vital time if things go wrong.

Check out the staff and headteacher carefully. If you like the headteacher, you're half-way there. They'll be your ally if things go wrong. Ask him/her what guarantees he can offer to ensure that your child will have good teachers – and what he will do if the teachers are not good enough.

Consider a 'faith-based' school for your child if you are comfortable about their approach to religion. Remember religious schools can be very tolerant and enlightened places.

Consider an Academy for your child but remember your child will have less rights at an Academy than in a LA controlled school. Academies are able to exclude children much more easily than other schools and Special Needs students appear to have less rights.

Consider a single-sex school for your child. Discuss the issues with your child. Remember that their feelings may change as they get older. Do also remember that statistics show pupils can achieve just as well in mixed-sexed schools.

Consider a specialist school for your child if that specialism is of interest to your child. Collect evidence and suitable referees. Encourage your child to join the musical and sporting groups on offer in your local area: many specialist schools favour musical and sporty children.

**Don't:**

Let your child carry the burden of your own anxiety; try to be as realistic and positive as you can.

Send your child to a school if you disagree with its philosophy or don't like its ethos.

Send your child to a school beset with discipline problems.

**What to do when your child doesn't get into their preferred school: APPEAL!!**

The government's announcement that parents who have not got their child into their first-choice school should appeal promises to cause mayhem in schools throughout the country – but that's not your problem. Clearly, the thing to do if you believe you have got a case and you are unhappy is appeal!

I should know about the chaos that happens because as a teacher in a top-achieving comprehensive in outer London, I've seen it all first-hand. In the past, parents, angry that their child has failed to gain a place, have phoned sobbing, shouted abuse at staff and, in one extreme case, staggered around drunk on the premises raging against the 'injustice' of the system.

I have spoken to a number of parents whose children have been rejected by popular schools. They all told me about their bitter disappointment. Most of them felt that their child's life would be harmed if he or she attended the school they had been offered. Many of them followed the government's current advice and appealed against the decision.

Then their fun really began. Mounting a 'school appeal' is a time-consuming and nerve-racking business. Furthermore, contrary to government propaganda, statistics show that it is often unproductive: roughly one fifth of appeals do not succeed. This is largely because many parents mount emotional appeals that their child needs a place because he likes the look of one school over another, or because his best friend goes to the school, or because he is too clever to go to a poorer-performing school.

These reasons will never succeed because they are not based on what are known as a school's 'admissions criteria', the rules by which it chooses its pupils – see above. If a parent's appeal is going to succeed, he or she must prove that the school did not apply its admissions criteria correctly or that the problems faced by the child in going to another school outweigh the trouble for the school in admitting the child.

Something to bear in mind is that a third of completed applications are faulty: forms are not filled in fully, vital questions are incorrectly answered, and crucial evidence is not provided. The net result may be that a child is not offered a place simply because bamboozled parents have not mastered the bureaucracy of the process. It is crucial to read the guidance issued by the school to the letter: one tiny slip-up can mean rejection.

Usually, the school or Local Authority website provides all the relevant details. Above all, your appeal will need to show that your child does indeed meet the school's admissions criteria. I have known parents measure the distance between the school and their home with rulers to show that they do indeed live within the catchment area. Other parents trying to get their child into faith-based schools pester their religious leaders for detailed references, in some cases attempting to butter them up with 'donations'. In one case, a parent actually pretended to be a pastor in order to get his child into a Christian school.

My advice is always to be honest but put absolutely everything you can think of into your appeal. This could mean showing that your child has aptitude in the school's 'specialisms', such as drama or sports, or that your child would benefit immeasurably from the unique curriculum the school offers, or that he has special educational needs that can only be catered for at your preferred school. With religious schools the requirements to be met can vary hugely, from just asking for evidence that you are practising in the particular faith, to demanding proof of regular church attendance for at least two years.

Appeals are not adjudicated by the school or LA, but independent people, usually drawn from the local community. They will consider all parents' points, including those not part of the school's admissions criteria. If there are 'special considerations' you will need to spell them out fully. I have known of parents who have confessed at appeal meetings that they are ill or disabled, which means their child needs to go to a school which is easily accessible by train or bus but not necessarily the closest school, and have succeeded with their appeal. The panel has the power to ignore a school's admissions criteria.

## CASE STUDY  A parent who took on the system and won

Jessica was in much the same position as many pupils living in the inner-city. She had attended a good primary school but was anxious about the move to secondary school. There was the choice of four schools: two mixed sexed comprehensives, a Christian girls' comprehensive and an Academy. Jessica really wanted to go to the Academy and took what she thought was an aptitude test for it. In fact, it wasn't the kind of test where the top scoring pupils were given places at all, but a banding test where the school sought to find equal numbers of top-achieving, middling and special needs pupils. Her second choice was the girls' comprehensive. Jessica was not offered a place at either school despite putting them top of the list. Instead, she was given a place at her third choice school, a mixed sexed comprehensive which had been judged to be 'satisfactory' by Ofsted and had a poor reputation in the area.

Jessica's mother, Lucy, decided to appeal against her rejection by the Academy. Taking advice from her LA Choice Advisor, Lucy listed absolutely everything that was relevant. Since the Academy specialised in the Arts and Media, Lucy included photocopied references of Jessica's drama teacher saying that Jessica had shown a marked aptitude for drama and had made her own film at school. She also included details about how Jessica had special education needs because of her dyslexia and that the Academy with its dyslexia unit could uniquely help with this. Furthermore, she pointed out that she herself had mobility problems and that the Academy was on a bus route that meant it was easily accessible for Jessica and herself.

One nerve-wracking morning, Lucy attended an appeal panel hearing. Two independent lay people listened to her case and examined all her documentation. A representative from the school tried to counter her claims. To her delight, Lucy's appeal succeeded. All her points were accepted as good reasons for Jessica to attend the school.

'It felt really scary,' Lucy told me. 'It felt like I had the might of the Academy against me. But the thing was that together with the Choice Advisor at the LA we were able to mount a good case. A water-tight case. We showed how Jessica's education would suffer if she went anywhere else.'

## CASE STUDY  A parent who took on the system and lost

Katie and Phil were adamant that their son, William, a shy, sensitive boy with an interest in collecting coins was not going to go to their local comprehensive, which was a notorious failing school. The school was enough to scare any parent: hardly a week went by when something unpleasant wasn't reported in the local press. Pupils had been caught carrying knives to school to protect themselves from bullying, one ex-member of staff had sued the school when a pupil who'd attacked him had not been expelled, and there had been a serious riot in which the police had been called to quell the chaos. So when William failed to get into the nearest Academy and was offered a place at the comprehensive, they appealed. Unfortunately, William was not good at sports, the specialism of the school, and did not fit any of the other criteria the Academy required to be met. The appeal failed. Katie and Phil were now desperate and decided to take the case to the Ombudsman, saying that the criteria of the Academy was unfair because it didn't cater for children like William who were not sporty. This too failed to make an impact.

In protest, Katie decided to keep William off school for a year rather than send him to the local comp. The Local Authority and the local press became involved and Katie was threatened with legal action for withholding her son from school. In the end, it was agreed that William would attend the local comp in Year 8. By then this failing school had a new headteacher, who was beginning to make an impact, sorting out the poor discipline and imposing more rigorous academic standards in the classroom. He took a special interest in William, making sure that he was placed in a suitable class and given work which would stretch him. Contrary to all their expectations, Katie and Phil found that William began to thrive in the school. It appeared that the poor behaviour was now limited to outside the classroom, and that it was mostly due to internecine warfare between rival gang members; as long as you weren't part of the gang you were okay. In the process, William got to know all the teenagers in his area and became much more confident and outgoing. Last year, he left the school with good GCSEs, and is now off to a Sixth Form college to study Sciences.

Katie and Phil still don't regret making such a fuss, though. Their very public refusal to let their son attend the school in Year 7 certainly contributed to the school getting a new head and it also meant that William received special treatment when he got to the school.

## Joining schools late: is it wise? Is it possible? How do you do it?

One way around the problem of not getting the school of your choice is to apply to it later on. Frequently, places come up at oversubscribed schools during term-time because pupils leave. This is how I got my son into an over subscribed primary school. When we had first applied, there wasn't a place for him because we didn't live close enough to the school. But when we applied again half-way through Year 4, there was room: pupils had left and there were spaces.

The problem, of course, is that you have to take the spot at a popular school as soon it comes up, even if it is during term time. You should look carefully again at the school before coming to any judgements, thinking carefully about the pros and cons. Generally, stability is best; you will need to have some good reasons for pulling your child out of their current school.

Questions to consider:

- Will my child be better taught at the new school?
- Will the new school help my child settle in?
- What happens if my child is bullied at the new school?
- Does the school have a clear bullying policy?
- What are the benefits of sending my child to the new school?
- What are the disadvantages?

If the benefits outweigh the disadvantages then go for it!

### Do:

Appeal if you haven't got the school you want.

Remember you must prove that you meet the school's admissions criteria and/or that the trouble your child will endure as a result of not going to the school will outweigh the trouble the school will have in admitting him or her.

Bear in mind many appeals are won when parents show that only their preferred school can uniquely meet their child's needs. This means doing some research into their policies.

Use all available advice lines/resources. Most Local Authorities have 'Choice Advisors' who will guide you through the process. If not, contact the Advisory Centre for Education (ACE) on 0808 800 5793 or http://www.ace-ed.org.uk who will help you too. Remember though this is not a simple process and you may find it confusing to receive two different sets of advice, so try the helplines one at a time.

Go to the Ombudsman if you fail at appeal. http://www.lgo.org.uk

Put your child on the waiting lists of preferred schools. You can always move them later, and this is not as traumatic as you might fear. Consider a switch if your child is suffering because of consistently poor teaching, bullying, being in an environment that is not conducive to learning. Consider switching at key moments such as at the end of Year 9 when your child is about to go in Year 10 and do GCSEs.

**Don't:**
Make a snap judgment based on prejudice. It may be that the school with a bad reputation actually has great teachers and a great atmosphere when you visit it.

Panic. Most schools are not that bad. Ultimately, it is your input which will decide your child's future, not the school.

Pay for advice. The best helplines (ACE and LA's advisors) are free.

Be suckered into spending hard-earned cash on school appeals.

## Working the System

Switch to a school you haven't researched thoroughly.
Keep switching schools. This can be very destabilising.

# School Involvement

*Your children need your presence more than your presents.* **Jesse Jackson**

**How do I help my child settle into his new school?**
Joining a new school is probably the most traumatic time for all students, whatever age. The best way to alleviate fears and anxieties is to be prepared.

First, make sure they have:

- The right uniform
- The right books and equipment
- Their timetable, the dates and times for term-time

Before the new term starts, ask for practical information from the school. Many schools have 'starter' packs for parents and child. If they don't, suggest they make one.

Such guides should include:

- A map of the school, including information on:

drinking fountains, toilets, washing basins, medical facilities, the phone

• Procedures for break and lunchtimes

• What to do if your child is ill: the school nurse, the medical facilities and procedures

• Important dates: the parents' evenings, concerts, jumble sales etc

• What the extra curricular activities are and how to get involved with them: the sports' fixtures and clubs, the other after-school and lunchtime clubs

• What to do if your child is unhappy in a lesson

• Complaints procedures and contact details of the governors, particularly the parent governor

### What do you do if the school can't provide this information?

Contact the headteacher: it is his or her responsibility to provide this information for you. If he or she does not oblige, you should inform your parent governor at the school. The school needs to improve its communications to parents!

### Should I become a school governor?

Governors of the school are the unpaid volunteers who make sure that the school is providing a good education for its pupils; ultimately they are responsible for supervising the staff and pupils in the school. This is not a small job! It's unpaid and frequently full of drama. Governors are not and should not be involved in the day-to-day running of the school, but they do have real power: they are involved in the appointment of many staff, including the headteacher, and they supervise the financing and structuring of the school. They are the people to go to if you have a serious complaint.

You should only become one if you have the time and commitment. However, the rewards are great, particularly if you have a pro-active governing body which takes a close interest in the school. You can really shape a school's future.

**Do:**
Consider being a governor if you have plenty of time and energy to spare.

You really want to help out.

**Don't:**
Be a governor if you don't have the time.

Be a governor if you hate paperwork.

Be a governor if you are a meddling busy-body. You'll come unstuck!

**For more information:**
Contact your child's school

http://www.sgoss.org.uk/home/individuals.htm

http://www.governornet.co.uk/

http://schools.london.anglican.org/Governors/governors-index.htm.

The London Diocesan Board for Schools (LDBS) runs excellent unbiased courses for governors.

Read *The Effective School Governor* (2001) by Joan Dean (Routledge, 2000).

## Should I set up a Parent Council?
This is a new idea that the government is very keen on; it wants to give parents the chance to set up their own group to give

advice to their child's school. They are less formal than governing bodies but in a way may be much more influential. They are designed so that parents can get involved in the nitty-gritty of learning in schools and give recommendations about how lessons and behaviour could be improved. They have yet to make a huge impact, having only been set up in May 2007.

**Do:**
Consider setting up or joining a council if you are worried about the teaching at your child's school.

**Don't:**
Join if you are not interested in having an impact in the classroom.

**For more information:**
Go to http://www.governornet.co.uk and look for the Parent Council pdf to download.


**Parent Associations (PAs), also known as Parent Teacher Associations (PTAs)**
PAs have no formal powers but they are important; they often fundraise for schools and hold popular social events. If you want to get involved with your child's school but can't face the hard work of being a governor, then becoming a member of the PA is the next best thing.

The key things to remember are:

• Even contributing a tiny bit helps.

• Don't assume that if a PA person approaches you in the playground, they are going to ask you to run a cake stand at the school fete – they might just ask for a little help, something that you can do easily, and usually they are tremendously organised!

- Be prepared for trouble ahead if you want to do something a bit different; schools are generally very conservative places.

- Fight for what you think is right: an active Parent Association is much more powerful than you think. Teachers do listen to them.

In Britain as a whole, PAs raise about £73 million a year. On average each PA raises about £5,600 per year for its school. They do make a real difference.

**Do:**
Become a PA member if you want to raise money for your child's school.

Become a PA member if you enjoy social events and activities, and like the idea of getting stuck into the school community.

**Don't:**
Join if what you really want to do is influence the teaching/curriculum at the school. Become a governor, or join a Parent Council instead.

**For more information about Parent Associations and how to go about setting one up at your school:** the website of National Confederation of Parent Teacher Association (NCPTA) – http://www.ncpta.org.uk

## Home-school agreements

Parents are usually asked to sign a document which is a formal agreement between the school and the parent setting out what is expected of the school, the parent and the pupil.

A home-school agreement usually contains:

- The school's overall aims and what it believes in

- What the school expects of its teachers and the standard

of discipline it expects of its pupils

• What support it expects from parents

Parents do NOT have to sign this agreement and it was made clear in the legislation that no child or parent should be punished for their failure or refusal to sign the agreement. Schools are not allowed to force parents to sign the agreement before they send their child to the school.


## School reports – what they really mean

Every school in the country is legally obliged to report upon all their pupils' progress in all National Curriculum subjects at least once a year. Many parents do not understand these reports because they are often written in the jargon of the subject and seem deeply impersonal.

The emphasis in these reports is not on comparing the child with other pupils in the class but on focusing upon his skills and establishing some targets he should work towards. Many schools use 'statement banks' in order to write their reports. This means that teachers select the statement that best fits the child rather writing an individualised comment. Even schools which don't do this inevitably produce reports which have an atmosphere of cut and paste about them. Burdened with writing exhaustive descriptions of what a child knows, many teachers opt to produce a 'stock report' which describes the content of the year and then fill in certain gaps where appropriate.

No wonder many parents end up feeling mystified and angry. They are bemused by the detailed statements and jargon used to catalogue their child's progress, and irritated by the fact that their child's report often looks very similar to many other reports that they have been sneaking a peek at.

Some schools have opted to abandon long reports altogether and to issue more regular – once every six weeks or so – progress checks where a pupils' grades and effort in each subject is reported upon, together with key targets for improvement. This seems to me eminently more sensible than long wordy reports that no one reads.

## A cynical teacher's view of school reports – and a more balanced perspective

Mr Duke, a former colleague of mine and grammar schoomaster throwback – bald, forthright, white moustache, flowing black gown – once told me what he perceived to be the truth about school reports. 'There was a time,' he said, 'when I could write such comments as "desperate", "a waste of space", "idiotic driveller" on school reports and not only get away with it, but be applauded. You see, positive comments mean nothing unless you are known for being negative when it's appropriate. But that's gone out of the window now! We have to be relentlessly, blandly, pointlessly upbeat. We're not allowed to say a spade is a spade anymore.' He produced a checklist of the euphemistic language teachers use in school reports with his own translations.

**Challenging behaviour** = an absolute bloody nightmare

**Fails to meet deadlines** = lazy bugger

**Finds the work challenging** = a bit thick

**Handwriting is difficult to decipher** = illiterate scrawl

**Inadequate preparation for lessons** = never does any homework

**Has learning difficulties** = unteachable

**Lively** = a pain in the arse

**Quiet in class** = never says a bloody word

**Reads slowly** = illiterate

**Reluctant to listen** = never shuts his trap

**Satisfactory progress** = isn't learning much

**Slow progress** = takes forever to do anything

**Sensitive to criticism** = touchy bugger

**Provocative comments** = rude bugger

**Talkative** = needs to put a sock in it

**Time-management issues** = timewaster

**Unsatisfactory progress** = might as well not bother turning up

Mr Duke's translations have a degree of truth, but they are not the whole story. The point is that school reports are almost blanketly positive now because they do aim to be motivational, to make a child aware of what they *can* do and what they need to work upon, rather than relentlessly focusing upon their failings. This is just good psychology. However, sometimes this can mean that the truth about what your child is getting up to in the classroom doesn't come out. If you are confused about their reports, or feel you can read a degree of tension between the lines, you should make an appointment to see the relevant teacher – or the head of year if you have any concerns. If, for example, your child does not seem to want to talk about school when at home, or appears never to have to do much homework, or is overburdened by too much of it – you need to try and get behind the euphemistic, upbeat language and find out what is really going on: to find out just how well your child is learning in the classroom, and what they need to do to improve.

**Do:**
Read through the reports with your child and see if they understand them.

Check to see your child is improving.

Talk through the things your child is doing right. This is very important, but often not done. Children need to know what they are doing right so that they can develop.

Try and find specific targets that are comprehensible. If you don't understand what your child needs to do to improve, you must ask.

Talk things through with the relevant teacher/head of year if you find your child's reports incomprehensible or lacking in vital details about how they could improve.

**Don't:**
Ignore the school reports entirely: they are important and need to be discussed with your child.

Be too cynical about the upbeat language: it serves an important purpose.

Become too emotional and start nagging or shouting threats.

**Parents' evenings**
If you have a serious problem, don't leave it to the Parents' evening to sort it out. Parents' evenings are always frenetic, emotional affairs where everyone is really uptight. They usually happen late in the afternoon after everyone has slogged through a stressful day and tempers can be fraught. The teachers are terrified of the barrage of complaints they might receive from the parents and the parents are petrified that their darlings might be criticised.

Teacher of the Year in 2004, Phil Beadle, offered this piece of advice for dealing with teachers at parents' evenings: 'The best way to speak to a teacher, if you want them to do something for your child, is nicely. If you bully me, your child's book goes to the bottom of the pile. This is a joke. But there is a valid point here. I don't get up at five thirty in the morning to mark books and prepare lessons, then deliver them with such energy and force that I am a wasted emotional shell at the end of term simply to be told I am not doing my job properly by some pushy parent.'

Sensible parents agree. Karen, a parent of children at a large, mixed comprehensive in Leeds, said: 'Show you are trying really hard to work out a problem with the teacher, rather then flouncing off after one conversation with them in search of the boss! There are ways of saying things, too. You might want to say 'You wanker, why can't you see that my child doesn't need constantly to be told what reading level she ought to be striving for.' Instead, you have to find a less pejorative and threatening route, such as 'We know Caroline very well, and we've found that setting a particular target for her is not helpful, as she naturally does her best, and that is all we would ever expect. Giving her numbers to chase is causing sleepless nights, which is not doing any of us any good.'

If parents want to get the best out of their child's teachers, they need to appear supportive, particularly if they sense that their teacher is a sensitive soul – as many are. Derek and Fiona told me the story of their child's primary school teacher who burst into tears when they suggested that their child wasn't learning much maths in the class.

'I am trying so hard, and I get no appreciation for what I am doing,' the teacher sobbed. 'I have slaved night and day over those maths worksheets and this is the thanks I get.' Derek now realizes that a less direct approach may have evinced a more satisfactory answer. 'I could tell she was on the edge by the way her hands were trembling,' he said. 'In the end, we had to reassure her that everything was fine – even when it wasn't! It was very embarrassing.'

Some schools try to fit far too much into their parents' evenings. Nicola, who has a son and daughter at a large comprehensive in a big town in Northumberland, explained to me why the parents' evening at their schools were terrible. 'At the beginning of the evening, you are given all your child's reports, with their baseline scores, their target scores and their actual scores. That leaves you with about three or four minutes to read at least 11 reports, digest all the statistical data on your child, and then talk to your child's teachers. It is impossible to feel informed about anything because you just can't absorb that amount of information in such a short space of time. I think the school does it because they don't trust the children to take the reports home, and they are too stingy to post them. Anyway, it leads to a most unsatisfactory evening where you basically listen to the teachers read the information that is on the report card in the few minutes that you get to talk to them.'

Other schools leave big gaps between the issuing of reports and the parents' evening. This can be equally mystifying because everyone has forgotten what was on the original report and can't really remember whether anything has changed since then.

**Do:**

Contact the relevant teachers before parents' evening if there is a big problem.

Come prepared, if you can, with your child's last report. Bring a notebook and pen to jot down key comments.

Remember the most important thing is to see whether your child has *improved.*

Set some specific, time-bound targets if he or she hasn't improved.

Be supportive. Always be the teacher's friend – even if you don't like them. Ask them how you can help. That way the teacher will like your child more, and be more willing to go the extra mile to help.

**Don't:**
Panic! If it's been a bad night, don't return and hit the roof.

Lose your cool if you don't like what a teacher is saying or you feel they are not listening to you. Nothing is more stressful for a child than hearing that their parent has let rip and blown their teacher up.

Take time to reflect and review your notes. Follow up, by talking to the teacher your child likes best: this may not be their form tutor.


## How much should I help my child with homework?

Homework is always a problem for parents; either their children are getting too much or too little; either it is too hard or too easy. Whatever teachers do, it's never right. There is strong evidence to suggest that homework can actually harm some children's progress; this is particularly the case when a child can't do the work. Frequently, they feel inadequate and become defensive and demotivated. Then they get into trouble for not doing it when all along they haven't really understood what to do. If this is happening, you will need to talk to your child about the problems they are having, then contact your child's teachers and find out what is going on. Keith and Clare from Killay in Swansea were angry about the amount of homework that their Year 7 child was being given and told me:

'Josh gets given homework on Monday, Wednesday and Friday, and then on top of that, he is given extra English and maths homework. It is very stressful for him to deal with this great mountain of work. He is in school for six hours a day: what's he doing in school if he is not doing work? We feel we are doing the teachers' jobs for them at home. I have to sit down with him and help him quite a bit. I listen to him read the books and we check his maths homework.'

The truth is a lot of parents can end up feeling like this about homework. I know I did when I did Blake's homework for him! He would come home with long worksheets to complete and no idea about how to do them. This is the wrong kind of homework.

The best homework is developmental: it is not just a repetition or extension of what goes on in the classroom but includes activities which are inspiring and challenging. The best kind of project work sets pupils discrete tasks to get on with over a few weeks on a related theme and can be really motivating. Primary schools are great at this, giving their pupils projects to do on their local area, on the environment, on famous people etc.

The best schools actually take a very broad view of homework: they believe it should be fun. For example, they might ask children to do some cooking with their parents, or have a conversation with them, or go to a park to observe the flora and fauna, or go to a museum.

**Top excuses for homework not being handed in – the ones I get sick of hearing!**

1 My printer broke…

2 I lost my book…

3 I didn't have any paper – or a pen…

4 I didn't know I had any – and my computer broke…

5 I didn't know the deadline was today…

6 My mum wasn't home last night…

7 My printer broke and my email was down…

8 I've got it all on a data-stick (Pupil then offers to print it out, but finds the data-stick is broken).

9  I was doing coursework, you know, REAL homework...

10  I would have done it if I'd understood it...

**Do:**

Remember that homework is not all about filling in work-sheets. The best homework could be helping your child plant some seeds, digging the weeds, doing some cooking, decorating their room, having a chat with you.

Provide the right conditions in which homework can be done. Do this by assisting with your child's organisation: give them a clear and definite place to work, some files or drawers to store their work, and, if necessary, help them organise their bag for the NEXT DAY. Many problems occur with children who are hurrying to get together their stuff in the morning, and are always forgetting things in the rush.

Encourage your child to do their homework by designating a time when EVERYONE does some work, including the parents. This could mean that you sit and read a book while your child does the homework. This is far better than you slinking off to watch the television while your poor kid works. The children who really struggle with school are the ones who have parents who they never see read or write at all. Homework time is the best time for a child to see their parent reading a book!

Check your facts first before complaining to the teacher. Is your child really telling you the truth about the homework that is being set? I've had parents fuming with me because I have supposedly not been setting any homework only to find out that their child had not been writing it down in their diary. This is particularly a problem with reading home-work which is difficult to monitor: many teachers have to assume against their better judgement that the reading has been done.

Celebrate the completion of good homework.

**Don't:**

Nag, nag, and nag about homework not done. Discuss your concerns with your child instead and set some clear targets.

These are the eminently sensible government guidelines about the amount of homework your child should be doing:

**Primary**

| | |
|---|---|
| Years 1 and 2 | 1 hour a week (reading, spelling, other literacy work and number work) |
| Years 3 and 4 | 1.5 hours a week (literacy and numeracy work, occasional assignments in other subjects) |
| Years 5 and 6 | 30 minutes a day (regular weekly schedule with continued emphasis on literacy and numeracy but also ranging widely over the curriculum) |

**Secondary**

| | |
|---|---|
| Years 7 and 8 | 45-90 minutes a day |
| Year 9 | One hour a day |
| Years 10 and 11 | 1.5-2.5 hours a day |

## Coursework nightmares

One of the biggest sources of conflict between parents and pupils
– and teachers for that matter – is coursework. Coursework is
work done either at school or at home in non-exam conditions as
part of the GCSE or A-level syllabus and frequently contributes
to the final grade a student gets, so it is particularly important. It
was originally introduced to try and make the exam system fairer
to those students who did not perform well under pressure, but it
has been beset with problems. The major problems include:

- Failure to meet deadlines

- Failure to do the work adequately
- Obsessive re-drafting
- Pupils expecting parents to write the coursework
- Plagiarism
- Cheating

In 2005, the Qualifications and Curriculum Authority (QCA)
published an extensive report into coursework which uncovered
that quite a bit of foul play was going on. In particular, pupils
were using the internet to copy and paste chunks of essays, pay
for tailor-made essays or hire online tutors to provide extensive,
individualised help. This report resulted in a whole-scale re-shaping
of GCSEs and A Levels, which promised to get rid of coursework as we know it. However, the upshot of this is that rather
than coursework being scaled back, it has actually increased – the
difference is that, as of September 2009, there is to be much less
work completed at home, and much more under the supervision of a teacher. QCA say this will lead to much better coursework tasks, which are tailored to the individualised needs of the
student. The new 'controlled conditions' coursework is aimed at
getting around the problem of on-line cheating. it will mean in
the large majority of cases that pupils bring in notes and research
material that they can refer to in class and then complete the

relevant tasks under the supervision of a teacher.[9] But quite how it will work in practice remains to be seen;

It could be very costly in terms of time and make teachers no more than glorified invigilators for much of the GCSE course. As for the old style of home-based coursework, where it is retained, the Office of the Qualifications and Examinations Regulator (Ofqual) has published a report for parents that lays out what they should and should not do: http://www.ofqual.gov. The report contains no surprises other than stating the bleeding obvious: don't write the coursework for your child, do encourage them to research the topic thoroughly, and keep an eye out for online cheating.

In theory, coursework should be great. It should give students the chance to go into a topic in real depth, conducting their own research and shaping their ideas in their own unique way; it should enable them to gain invaluable feedback from their teacher and peers, and produce a finished draft which is an embodiment of all that they've learnt. Unfortunately, the reality is very, very different: many parents who want their children to achieve great results actually write the coursework for them, or take steps to make sure the relevant family friend does. I have a feeling that with 'controlled conditions' work, the situation will remain much the same because pupils will be able to bring in their own notes. This will effectively mean that the children of pushy parents will have a sheaf of special notes which will contain their ticket to top marks. What is more, it looks as though 'controlled conditions' coursework at GCSE will count for even more of the final marks than coursework did under the old system.

Now some schools may well police these controlled conditions sessions rigorously, confiscating all notes that they view as too 'helpful' – notes which effectively write the essay for

---

9  http://www.ofqual.gov.uk/files/qca-07-3208_controlledassessmentfinal3.pdf

the student. But many schools, I bet you, will not confiscate overly helpful notes for the simple reason that schools are under the cosh to get great results. Many schools I've taught in covertly encourage their pupils to cheat by either commanding pupils to submit work that is of higher quality – or not at all. I've seen teachers put lines through honest but poor work, with the comment: 'This needs to be completely re-written as a good essay.' This sort of comment sends pupils scrambling in a panic back to their parents, many of whom help their children extensively with the coursework. Some misguided but well-meaning teachers mark pupils' work so closely that they are effectively writing it for the child. The trouble is that teachers are often obliged to meet 'quotas' of grades; in one school I was told that I had to get 100% A*-C grades for my pupils, even though nearly half of them were D and E grade students. The only way to solve this problem was either to write the coursework for the pupils, or give them a 'scaffold' for the essay which was so detailed that they could hardly fail to write a passable essay.

So where does this leave parents? I think sensible parents should be the voices of sanity amidst this madness. They should insist that their children do their own work and should complain if they feel a teacher is completing the coursework for their child. After all, all this cheating may boost a child's results in the short-term but in the long-term it gives a child a totally false picture of their abilities: sooner or later they are going to come a cropper when they have to do some work of their own.

Parents should be aware of the terrible signal they are sending to their child if they do the coursework for them. They're basically saying: 'I care more about you getting an A grade than I do about you doing your own work.' Now, it may be that you feel that your child deserves an A grade and you can see that he or she is not getting anywhere near that in their coursework. In which case, you can legitimately complain that your child is underachieving and ask what steps can be taken to help them improve. The honest path is a far better strategy in the long run – even from a very selfish perspective – because the bottom line is that writing your child's coursework for them won't help them pass the relevant exams, which still count for a lot of marks: usually over 50% of marks at GCSE, and 60% at A Level. To do well, your child is going to need to pass a few exams without any help from Mum and Dad. They actually need to learn to work independently and, if they do their own work for the coursework, they will be in a much better position to do so.

## CASE STUDY A parent who wrote her son's coursework

Jenny was most anxious that her son, Jack, should achieve top results and study a subject such as law and medicine at university. From an early age, she'd always pushed Jack to do activities which would make him stand out as a talented boy: she employed a Maths tutor, made him go to ballet lessons, and learn several musical instruments. Jenny would have liked him to have attended a grammar school, but there were none in the local area and instead Jack attended the local comprehensive, which, being in an affluent area, was a high-achieving school with plenty of children from similar backgrounds to Jack. Unfortunately, Jenny felt that the 'slack' atmosphere of the school affected Jack adversely: he soon gave up learning his musical instruments, his ballet lessons and refused to be tutored further. Instead he enjoyed playing his guitar with friends and became a stereotypically bolshy teenager who was underachieving at school. Jenny nagged him about his work constantly, comparing him to the bright, ambitious child he used to be, and the sullen creature he was now. This led to furious rows.

By the time, Jack was doing his GCSE courses, he was a law unto himself. Jenny hardly ever saw him do any homework and only learnt about the coursework he needed to do at a Year 10 parents' evening. Horrified, but seeing that he might still have a chance of attaining the grades she hoped he would get, she cajoled and nagged him into showing her what he had to do. She then set about 'working with him': this invariably meant doing the work herself while he grunted at her that what she was doing was 'OK'. He was grateful for the work she did and became more compliant as a result: he was aware that he was in her debt.

The coursework achieved top grades and enabled Jack to scrape through his GCSEs and do A Levels in Maths, Physics, Biology and English Literature, all the subjects that Jenny hoped he might do. However, Jack couldn't last the course with these A Levels: they were too difficult for him and he ended up being forced to drop them. He then left the comprehensive altogether and went to a college where he did A Levels in Music Production, Music and IT. Jenny's plans for Jack had backfired – and she came to realise that her help with the coursework had actually made Jack 'lose' a year because his coursework marks had artificially inflated his results and the school's expectations of him.

In the end, Jenny's 'involvement' with the coursework prevented Jenny and Jack from thinking about what he really wanted to do and the root causes of his disaffection with school and his work. In retrospect, Jenny realises that she would have been better off addressing these concerns at the time instead of putting so many hours of legwork into doing Jack's coursework for him.

**Do:**
Encourage your child to do their own work.

To do some research of their own. Go to galleries, museums, sites of interest.

Encourage your child to meet their deadlines.

Complain if the coursework isn't marked promptly.

**Don't:**
Write the coursework for them.

Pay for a private tutor/internet site to write the coursework.

Complain if your child's teacher won't endlessly re-mark their work

**Should I hire a private tutor for my child?**
In an ideal world where all state school teachers were perfect, you should never have to hire a private tutor. But the reality is that sometimes you may have to consider this. In my experience, most state schools are pretty good on the arts subjects but struggle to find really good maths and science teachers. If your child is falling behind with maths, then it is well worth considering getting some extra help.

You must make sure that your tutor is properly qualified and is able to teach the correct syllabus. I have come across a number of children whose parents have hired private tutors that have been worse than useless because they have taught the wrong syllabus!

**Do:**
Demand extra help from your child's school before going down this route. Complain about poor teaching if necessary (see section: **How do I make my child's ropey teachers better?**)

Talk to your child's school and find out their attitude before you hire the tutor. Some schools actively encourage them, others do not. You will need to make your own judgements about these attitudes but you should be very wary of schools that are virtually blackmailing you to get a tutor to disguise their own faults.

Discuss the decision to hire a tutor with your child. You must get his or her enthusiastic agreement. If you can, talk to your child's teacher and see what he thinks. Ask for the syllabus they are studying and copies of previous exam papers: you are entitled to do this. It may be that you can help your child yourself and save yourself the money.

Be wary of teachers at your child's school who are touting for extra money. Many teachers run revision lessons free of charge, recognising the need for these lessons.

Ask to see the tutors' qualifications yourself, including their passport, two reputable referees and a Criminal Records Bureau (CRB) check. All qualified teachers in Britain have to have such a document which proves they have no criminal convictions, and all private tutors should produce one. Don't trust the agency you have signed up with to do this unless they EXPLICITLY say that they do it. Ask the tutor how familiar they are with the syllabus your child is studying and what relevant resources they have to offer. The internet has a whole host of different private tutoring sites.

Set some measurable, time-bound targets with the tutor. For example, they should help your child attain a 'B' grade in their next English exam.

**Don't:**
Force your child to have a private tutor. If you really feel strongly that he or she needs one, talk him/her around with persuasive arguments, pointing out that you only want the best for him/her. Don't threaten or bribe. Set up a decent 'points' system instead.

Expect miracles. Set achievable targets instead.

Be bullied into getting a tutor, however if your child has a learning difficulty they should receive extra funding and help from the school (see SEN section). Equally, if the teaching in your child's school is sub-standard you need to address this matter urgently with the Headteacher and, if necessary, the governing body.

# Learning

*What we want to see is the child in
pursuit of knowledge, not knowledge in pursuit
of the child.* **George Bernard Shaw**

## What Your Child Should Learn At School

At the heart of everything your child learns at school is the
National Curriculum. The dreaded, loathed, despised, pillo-
ried, ridiculed National Curriculum. In recent years, it's gone
through a radical overhaul, supposedly making it more engaging, flexible and in tune with the modern world. As you may
have read in the press, the 'overhaul' hasn't been very satisfactory: much of the content of the curriculum has been stripped
away – by and large pupils are not required to remember facts
and figures anymore – and has been replaced with a requirement
for pupils to learn 'skills'. The Qualifications and Curriculum
Authority (QCA) which is in charge of developing the National Curriculum and the assessment regime that accompanies it
says that the new National Curriculum aims to produce:

- Successful learners who enjoy learning, make progress and achieve
- Confident individuals who are able to live safe, healthy and fulfilling lives
- Responsible citizens who make a positive contribution to society

The first aim is entirely admirable and comprehensible but the next two, to produce 'confident individuals' who lead 'fulfilling lives' and to develop 'responsible citizens' who make a 'positive contribution' are very vague and beg all sorts of questions. What is a responsible citizen? One that does everything the government asks them to do? And is it really the responsibility of school to execute this?

I am afraid this sort of woolliness runs right through the National Curriculum, bleeding into every sentence. You need to make the best of it you can.

## What is in the National Curriculum?

The NC sets out what subjects are to be taught; the knowledge, skills and understanding required in each subject; the standards or attainment targets in each subject that enable your child's progress is properly measured; and how your child's progress is assessed and reported. It is organised into blocks of years called 'key stages' which are as follows:

**Key Stage 1** – 5-7 year olds (Years 1-2)

**Key Stage 2** – 7-11 year olds (Years 3-6)

**Key Stage 3** – 11-14 year olds (Years 7-9)

**Key Stage 4** – 14-16 year olds (Years 10-11)

**Key Stage 5** – 16-18 year olds (Years 12-13)

**The values of the National Curriculum**

From 2002 to 2007, the government re-evaluated the curriculum stating that schools should nurture:

**The self** – enabling students to grow spiritually, morally, intellectually

**Relationships** – teaching children to value each other

**Diversity in our society** – valuing freedom, justice, human rights, the rule of law and collective effort

**The environment** – making sure we protect it

**For more, log onto:** http://curriculum.qca.org.uk/

**What you need to know about the compulsory subjects in the National Curriculum: an important survival guide**

There are some common themes that are reinforced in subject after subject, in Key Stage after Key Stage. These are:

**Literacy skills** – understanding words and grammar (i.e being able to make an argument or structure a piece of writing effectively.)

**Numeracy skills** – the practical use of number and maths in every day situations

**Analysing texts and data**

**The difference between facts and opinions**

**Investigative methods**

The compulsory subjects in the National Curriculum are important, but there is a general feeling, even in the teaching profession, that they are not extensive enough. If a subject is not compulsory, then many schools will not bother much with it. Most troubling for the concerned parent is the lack of compulsory requirements for certain academic subjects: modern foreign languages and the humanities at Key Stage 4. This means if you are not careful your child may not take GCSEs in these subjects; indeed some schools may not even offer them because their resources have been redirected to offering diplomas and vocational GCSEs. But the bottom line is: no top university will seriously consider a student for a popular course such as law or medicine unless they have at least five good A*/A grades at GCSE.

That means you need to make sure your child is doing at least five respected GCSEs. These are:

- English language
- English literature (this may become an option in the future so watch out for this)
- Maths
- Science
- A modern foreign language
- A humanities subject such as geography, history or religious education

In our current national educational set-up, the most important thing to focus on are your child's GCSEs. These remain the most important qualifications because they effectively determine your child's future.

If I were to give a short game plan to every parent in the country, it would be this:

- 0-14 years: make sure your child is motivated, happy, can read and write fluently, is pretty good at maths and has good working habits. Don't push too hard, but make sure they're not lazy slobs.

- 14-16 years: really think strategically about training your child to get top grades at GCSE. Have a long talk with them about how they are going to achieve this. Push your child's teachers for extra work if necessary. Have high expectations.

• 16-18 years: be aware that the top universities favour some A-levels over others. For example, there is no chance that you will become a medic unless you do three sciences, and usually maths. For competitive degrees such as law, you will need to show you have done 'serious' A Levels such as: English Literature (not Language), History or Geography, Maths, Economics, one of the Sciences. Bear in mind that other A-levels such as Drama, Media, Psychology, Sociology, are not so highly regarded by the top universities. By all means choose one of these as a fourth A-level, or one just to take to AS-level but make sure that the other A-Levels are highly regarded. It is very important that you have an honest talk with a knowledgeable teacher about this. Be aware that you may be given false information as some teachers might be keen to fill up courses that are not so popular. If in doubt, call the Oxbridge admissions office to find out what they take seriously, and use this as a benchmark.

• 18-21 years: this is when young people go to university or get a job. Be aware there is a two-tier system with universities. The ones in the top 20 of the league tables are taken much more seriously by employers. There is a certain prejudice that all the old polys that are now universities are rubbish, but this is not the case at all. Some new universities have gained very high reputations in certain subjects. For example the University of East London has a very good reputation in Psychology, but you need to look carefully at the department that your child will be doing their degrees in – find out about their reputation for research and teaching. As a general rule, however, the older universities *are* more highly regarded, and for good reason.

**Are there any little known tips that might help my child with achieving highly?**

So far we've covered the obvious points that will greatly help your child achieve at school – such as encouraging them to read for pleasure, getting them to write a diary, assisting them in the right way with their homework.

There are also some basic tips that can help your child in all their work. These can be broken down into: study skills – often called 'learning to learn' in schools now – and language skills.

## Study Skills

Study skills are still badly taught in schools but it seems to me that this is one of the most key areas for your child to be proficient in: organising their thoughts, figuring out how and why they learn, presenting and sequencing information.

**Do:**

Help your child get organised. On the computer, help him or her put their documents into the relevant folders. And help him file his work; give him some space in your filing cabinet or a shelf in his room to put files.

Give him a noticeboard to put notices on.

Buy him a calendar to put his dates on.

Help him to learn how to take notes effectively, by pointing out that key words need to be noted down, not everything! And, when it comes to revising for tests or exams, help them to summarise their work, produce flashcards with the key points, and so on.

Teach your child how to do spider-diagrams. A spider-diagram involves placing the key topic for consideration in the centre of a page, and then using sub-topics to form branches from it. These sub-topics can in turn have branches – and so on. This can also be called Mind Mapping, a term invented by Tony Buzan – a more complex version of essentially the same thing. For more see: http://www.buzanworld.com or http://www.learningtolearn.group.shef.ac.uk/intro/index.html

**Don't:**
Nag, nag, nag about their poor organisation. Help them do something about it.

Be impatient! It's difficult, particularly when you are starting out.

## Language Skills
One of the best ways of improving your child's vocabulary is teaching them a little basic Latin and Greek. So much of our language is based on these two language families.

Does your child know what the following Latin and Greek prefixes mean?

'ante'
'bene'
'circum'
'demo'
'homo'
'omni'
'vita'[10]

If not, I would strongly recommend that you buy two great books that make the subject fun and racy. *Amo, Amas, Amat…and All That: How to Become a Latin Lover* by Harry Mount and *It's All Greek To Me* by Charlotte Higgins.

This website is also good for getting the basics: http://www.virtualsalt.com/roots.htm For more advice on improving vocabu-

---

10  The answers are, in this order: before, well, around, people, same, all, life

lary see: http://ezinearticles.com/?expert=Celia_Webb For more on Latin and Greek courses – and a whole host of other courses, look at the links here: http://www.word2word.com/coursead. html

## The National Curriculum Levels

These are the levels that measure your child's attainment at each Key Stage. If used sensibly, they can be a tremendous help to you, your child and your child's teachers because they give you a good idea about where your child is in relation to the rest of the country.

**At Key Stage 1**, by the age of 7, most children are expected to achieve a level 2 in reading, writing and maths.

**At Key Stage 2**, by the age of 11, most children are expected to achieve level 4 in English, maths and science.

**At Key Stage 3**, by the age of 14, most children are expected to achieve a level 6 in all of the National Curriculum subjects (see below for list)

**At Key Stage 4**, by the age of 16 , most children are expected to achieve 5 A*-C grades at GCSE, including English and Maths.

## The following subjects must be studied for the Key Stage 1 curriculum:

**Art and design**
**Design and technology**
**English**
**Geography**
**History**
**ICT**
**Mathematics**

**Music**
**Physical education**
**Science**

These subjects are optional, but usually covered by most schools:

**Citizenship**
**Personal, Social and Health Education**
**Religious Education** (It must be covered but there are no precise instructions about how it should be covered)

By the time they are seven, at Key Stage 1, your child should be getting Level 2s or more in English and maths. Check to see if he or she can reach this level by having a chat with them and their teachers about the criteria for the levels, which are outlined below, and whether your child fulfils them. If your child isn't attaining Level 2, ask for an Individual Action Plan to help your child attain the national average standard expected at this age.

**What is expected for English Level 2 – Speaking and Listening**
Pupils begin to show confidence in talking and listening, particularly where the topics interest them. On occasions, they show awareness of the needs of the listener by including relevant detail. In developing and explaining their ideas they speak clearly and use a growing vocabulary. They usually listen carefully and respond with increasing appropriateness to what others say. They are beginning to be aware that in some situations a more formal vocabulary and tone of voice should be used.

**What is expected for English Level 2 – Reading**
Pupils' reading of simple texts shows understanding and is generally accurate. They express opinions about major events or ideas in stories, poems and non-fiction. They use more than one strategy – such as phonic, graphic, syntactic and contextual – in reading unfamiliar words and establishing meaning.

**What is expected for English Level 2 – Writing**

Pupils' writing communicates meaning in both narrative and non-narrative forms, using appropriate and interesting vocabulary, and showing some awareness of the reader. Ideas are developed in a sequence of sentences, sometimes demarcated by capital letters and full stops. Simple, monosyllabic words are usually spelt correctly, and where there are inaccuracies the alternative is phonetically plausible. In handwriting, letters are accurately formed and consistent in size.

**What is expected for Level 2 in maths – Using and applying mathematics**

Pupils select the mathematics they use in some classroom activities. They discuss their work using mathematical language and are beginning to represent it using symbols and simple diagrams. They can explain why an answer is correct.

**What is expected for Level 2 in maths – Numbers and algebra**

Pupils count sets of objects reliably, and use mental recall of addition and subtraction facts to ten. They begin to understand the place value of each digit in a number and use this to order numbers up to 100. They choose the appropriate operation when solving addition and subtraction problems. They use the knowledge that subtraction is the inverse of addition. They use mental calculation strategies to solve number problems involving money and measures. They recognise sequences of numbers, including odd and even numbers.

**What is expected for Level 2 in maths – Shapes, space and measures**

Pupils use mathematical names for common 3-D and 2-D shapes and describe their properties, including numbers of sides and corners. They distinguish between straight and turning movements, understand angle as a measurement of turn, and recognise right angles in turns. They begin to use everyday non-standard and standard units to measure length and mass.

### What is expected for Level 2 in maths – Handling data

Pupils sort objects and classify them using more than one criterion. When they have gathered information, pupils record results in simple lists, tables and block graphs, in order to communicate their findings.

## The following subjects must be studied for the Key Stage 2 curriculum:

**Art and design**
**Design and technology**
**English**
**Geography**
**History**
**ICT**
**Mathematics**
**Music**
**Physical Education**
**Science**

These subjects are non-statuory, but usually covered by most schools:

**Citizenship**
**Personal, Social and Health Education**
**Modern Foreign Languages**
**Religious Education** (It must be covered but there are no precise instructions about how it should be covered)

The average score for a pupil at this stage is a Level 4. The criteria for attaining this level are outlined below. Again, if your child isn't set to attain a Level 4, ask for an Individual Action Plan.

### What is expected for Level 4 in English – Speaking and Listening

Pupils talk and listen with confidence in an increasing range of contexts. Their talk is adapted to the purpose: developing ideas thoughtfully, describing events and conveying their opinions clearly. In discussion, they listen carefully, making contributions and asking questions that are responsive to others' ideas and views. They use appropriately some of the features of Standard English vocabulary and grammar.

### What is expected for Level 4 in English – Reading

In responding to a range of texts, pupils show understanding of significant ideas, themes, events and characters, beginning to use inference and deduction. They refer to the text when explaining their views. They locate and use ideas and information.

### What is expected for Level 4 in English – Writing

Pupils' writing in a range of forms is lively and thoughtful. Ideas are often sustained and developed in interesting ways and organised appropriately for the purpose of the reader. Vocabulary choices are often adventurous and words are used for effect. Pupils are beginning to use grammatically complex sentences, extending meaning. Spelling, including that of polysyllabic words that conform to regular patterns, is generally accurate. Full stops, capital letters and question marks are used correctly, and pupils are beginning to use punctuation within the sentence. Handwriting style is fluent, joined and legible.

### What is expected for Level 4 in maths – Using and applying mathematics

Pupils are developing their own strategies for solving problems and are using these strategies both in working within mathematics and in applying mathematics to practical contexts. They present information and results in a clear and organised way. They search for a solution by trying out ideas of their own.

## What is expected for Level 4 in maths – Numbers and algebra

Pupils use their understanding of place value to multiply and divide whole numbers by 10 or 100. In solving number problems, pupils use a range of mental methods of computation with the four operations, including mental recall of multiplication facts up to 10 x 10 and quick derivation of corresponding division facts. They use efficient written methods of addition and subtraction and of short multiplication and division. They add and subtract decimals to two places and order decimals to three places. In solving problems with or without a calculator, pupils check the reasonableness of their results by reference to their knowledge of the context or to the size of the numbers. They recognise approximate proportions of a whole and use simple fractions and percentages to describe these. Pupils recognise and describe number patterns, and relationships including multiple, factor and square. They begin to use simple formulae expressed in words. Pupils use and interpret coordinates in the first quadrant.

## What is expected for Level 4 in maths – Shapes, space and measures

Pupils make 3-D mathematical models by linking given faces or edges, draw common 2-D shapes in different orientations on grids. They reflect simple shapes in a mirror line. They choose and use appropriate units and instruments, interpreting, with appropriate accuracy, numbers on a range of measuring instruments. They find perimeters of simple shapes and find areas by counting squares.

What is expected for Level 4 in maths – Handling data

Pupils collect discrete data and record them using a frequency table. They understand and use the mode and range to describe sets of data. They group data, where appropriate, in equal class intervals, represent collected data in frequency diagrams and interpret such diagrams. They construct and interpret simple line graphs.

## The following subjects must be studied for the Key Stage 3 curriculum:

**Art and design**
**Citizenship**
**Design and technology**
**English**
**Geography**
**History**
**ICT**
**Mathematics**
**Modern Foreign Languages**
**Music**
**Physical Education**
**Science**
**Personal, Social and Health Education** (Non-statuory, but usually covered by most schools)
**Religious Education** (Must be covered but there are no precise instructions about how it should be covered)

The national average score is Level 6 at Key Stage 3. In other words, your child should be attaining a Level 6 in all subjects. See below for what is expected of them at this stage.

## What is expected for Level 6 in English – Speaking and Listening

Pupils adapt their talk to the demands of different contexts with increasing confidence. Their talk engages the interest of the listener through the variety of its vocabulary and expression. Pupils take an active part in discussion, showing understanding of ideas and sensitivity to others. They are usually fluent in their use of Standard English in formal situations.

**What is expected for Level 6 in English – Reading**
In reading and discussing a range of texts, pupils identify different layers of meaning and comment on their significance and effect. They give personal responses to literary texts, referring to aspects of language, structure and themes in justifying their views. They summarise a range of information from different sources.

**What is expected for Level 6 in English – Writing**
Pupils' writing often engages and sustains the reader's interest, showing some adaptation of style and register to different forms, including using an impersonal style where appropriate. Pupils use a range of sentence structures and varied vocabulary to create effects. Spelling is generally accurate, including that of irregular words. Handwriting is neat and legible. A range of punctuation is usually used correctly to clarify meaning, and ideas are organised into paragraphs.

**What is expected for Level 6 in maths – Using and applying mathematics**
Pupils carry through substantial tasks and solve quite complex problems by independently breaking them down into smaller, more manageable tasks. They interpret, discuss and synthesise information presented in a variety of mathematical forms. Pupils' writing explains and informs their use of diagrams. Pupils are beginning to give mathematical justifications.

**What is expected for Level 6 in maths – Numbers and algebra**
Pupils order and approximate decimals when solving numerical problems and equations [for example, $3x + x = 20$], using

trial and improvement methods. Pupils are aware of which number to consider as 100 per cent, or a whole, in problems involving comparisons, and use this to evaluate one number as a fraction or percentage of another. They understand and use the equivalences between fractions, decimals and percentages, and calculate using ratios in appropriate situations. They add and subtract fractions by writing them with a common denominator. When exploring number sequences, pupils find and describe in words the rule for the next term or nth term of a sequence where the rule is linear. They formulate and solve linear equations with whole-number coefficients. They represent mappings expressed algebraically, and use Cartesian coordinates for graphical representation interpreting general features.

## What is expected for Level 6 in maths – Shapes, space and measures

Pupils recognise and use common 2-D representations of 3-D objects. They know and use the properties of quadrilaterals in classifying different types of quadrilateral. They solve problems using angle and symmetry properties of polygons and angle properties of intersecting and parallel lines, and explain these properties. They devise instructions for a computer to generate and transform shapes and paths. They understand and use appropriate formulae for finding circumferences and areas of circles, areas of plane rectilinear figures and volumes of cuboids when solving problems. They enlarge shapes by a positive whole-number scale factor.

## What is expected for Level 6 in maths – Handling data

Pupils collect and record continuous data, choosing appropriate equal class intervals over a sensible range to create frequency tables. They construct and interpret frequency diagrams. They construct pie charts. Pupils draw conclusions from scatter diagrams, and have a basic understanding of correlation.

When dealing with a combination of two experiments, pupils identify all the outcomes, using diagrammatic, tabular or other forms of communication. In solving problems, they use their knowledge that the total probability of all the mutually exclusive outcomes of an experiment is 1.

**The following subjects must be studied for the Key Stage 4 curriculum:**

**Citizenship**
**English**
**ICT**
**Mathematics**
**Physical Education**
**Science**
**Personal, Social and Health Education** (Non-statuory, but covered by most schools)
**Religious Education** (Must be covered but there are no precise instructions about how it should be covered)

Personally, I think when your child is 14, this is the time to sit down with them and have a chat about their future. They should be aiming for the very top. That said, you should make it clear that you're not going to be angry with him or her if they don't make it there. Teenagers need to feel it is their choice – because it is! They can choose to work hard or not. If they do work hard, then they are capable of getting the top grades. In particular, they should aim to do their very best in English and maths.

**To get an A grade in English:**
In a range of contexts, candidates select and use appropriate styles and registers. They vary their sentence structure, vocabulary and expression confidently for a range of purposes. They sustain discussion through the use of a variety of con-

tributions, listening with sensitivity. They show assured use of Standard English in a range of situations and for a variety of purposes. Candidates articulate and sustain their responses to texts, developing their ideas and referring in detail to aspects of language, structure and presentation. They identify and analyse argument, opinion and alternative interpretations, making cross-references where appropriate. They make apt and careful comparison within and between texts. Candidates' writing has shape and assured control of a range of styles. Narratives use structure as well as vocabulary for a range of effects and non-fiction is coherent, logical and persuasive. A wide range of grammatical constructions is used accurately. Punctuation and spelling are correct; paragraphs are well constructed and linked to clarify the organisation of the writing as a whole.

## To get an A grade in maths:

Candidates give reasons for the choices they make when investigating within mathematics itself or when using mathematics to analyse tasks: these reasons explain why particular lines of enquiry or procedures are followed and others rejected. Candidates apply the mathematics they know in familiar and unfamiliar contexts. Candidates use mathematical language and symbols effectively in presenting a convincing reasoned argument. Their reports include mathematical justifications, explaining their solutions to problems involving a number of features or variables. Candidates manipulate simple surds (square roots). They determine the bounds of intervals. Candidates understand and use direct and inverse proportion. They manipulate algebraic formulae, equations and expressions, finding common factors and multiplying two linear expressions. In simplifying algebraic expressions, they use rules of indices for negative and fractional values. They solve problems using intersections and gradients of graphs. Candidates sketch the graphs of sine, cosine and tangent functions for any angle and generate and interpret graphs based on these functions. Candidates use sine, cosine and tangent of angles of any size, and Pythagoras' theorem when solving problems in two and three dimensions. They use the conditions for congruent triangles in formal geometric proofs. They calculate lengths of circular arcs and areas of sectors, and calculate the surface area of cylinders and volumes of cones and spheres. They understand and use the effect of enlargement on areas and volumes of shapes and solids. Candidates interpret and construct histograms. They understand how different methods of sampling and different sample sizes may affect the reliability of conclusions drawn; they select and justify a sample and method, to investigate a population. They recognise when and how to work with probabilities associated with independent and mutually exclusive events.

## What every parent should know about maths in British schools

Britain desperately needs more mathematicians. Our economy depends upon the subject, more than any other. Every aspect of technology – from mobile phones, to the internet, to washing machines – requires mathematicians to design and make them. However, it looks increasingly like it won't be British students who will be at the technological forefront. The number of A-level maths students has slumped by nearly a third since the 1980s. There is also a severe shortage of qualified maths teachers, with one in five maths teachers not having a degree in the subject.

Simon Singh, the populist scientist who recently spent a week in school teaching maths for Teachers' TV, is very pessimistic about the state of affairs. 'The state of science and maths teaching in this country is catastrophic,' he says. 'And I'm not sure that there is anyone in government who is taking it seriously enough. We need to inject some passion into lessons, but most people are just so lack-lustre.'[11] Singh's comments are backed up by Ofsted, which recently found that nearly half of maths lessons were not good enough, being taught either by non-specialists or teachers too intent upon teaching to the test and not instilling genuine understanding.[12]

One reason often cited as to why there are less mathematicians is that the subject is too difficult. And yet, it is a lot easier than it used to be, when many more students were studying it at A Level. Tim Smith, a longstanding head of maths, at a top comprehensive in the south of England explained to me why this is so: 'In the days of the O-Level, the exam was designed for only about the top twenty per cent of students. This was not satisfactory, and so they introduced the GCSE, which was aimed at including everyone. The old O-Level required quite a sophisticated knowledge of algebra but this has been simplified considerably; and other areas previously covered like calculus have been removed. There is a further change coming about in GCSE maths, the result of an effort to make maths more *relevant.* A large proportion of the exam papers will be asking mathematical questions about such things as wallpapering a room, laying a carpet, going shopping, and supervising personal finances. The reason why maths is so unpopular with many kids is because they don't see why they have to do it. Hopefully, this will improve the situation.

So are maths teachers getting worse? Tim Smith swallowed hard before telling me the truth: 'There is no doubt that people who come into maths teaching now have not had the rigorous training that older mathematicians had. It does mean that for A-Level teaching you have got teachers who have not got the

11   *The Education Guardian* 27th October 2006 John Crace

12   http://www.telegraph.co.uk/education/3362385/Teacher-crisis-in-maths-and-science.html

depth of understanding that they once had. That sounds awful but it is true. I can recall many times over the last twenty years when I have found myself explaining key mathematical concepts to staff. This is because they have gone through the GCSE system and the new revised A-Level and just don't have the subject knowledge that someone who did the old O-level and A-Level would have had. Someone going through the new system is not required to prove things mathematically in the way that we were. The A-Level now is, in general, more superficial. Depending on the type of university they've been to, maths graduates have varying experiences. At the top flight universities, it is still rigorously mathematical. But there is no end of possibilities with degrees now: maths with economics, maths with psychology and so on and so forth. Somebody who has done one of these joint degrees won't have the mathematical grounding to teach the hardest parts of A-Level. There have always been shortages of maths teachers. When we advertised for six consecutive weeks in the late 1980s for a maths teacher, it didn't attract one applicant. We had to get somebody from an agency. This is the experience up and down the country. A good maths graduate ends up in accountancy, banking, commerce, the City, or an actuarial position. It is an excellent degree to have if you want to make money.'

I asked Tim why in the Far East, the maths teaching seemed to produce much better results from the students? He explained: 'In the Far East, young children are doing drill and learning by rote. The kids here rarely do things like that because it is so frowned upon by the educational establishment. You'd fail your Ofsted if you were observed doing mathematical drill. But in China, there is a lot of rote learning and drill, and as a result the processes of arithmetic and algebra come to be second nature to children as young as six, seven and eight years old. In China, a lot of the teaching is perhaps regarded as archaic and formulaic, and stifling of creativity and free thinking. Nevertheless, it does seem to produce a lot of very competent mathematicians. They may not have the flexibility of thought of our students, but they certainly have a lot more knowledge.'

**Do:**

Talk to your child's maths teacher. He will have a whole host of statistics and ideas that he can talk through with you.

Have a basic knowledge of the National Curriculum requirements (see above) and give your children little tests on what they know.

Give your child some revision guides to work through. These days there are no end of aids to help with maths. A whole industry has sprung up on the back of angst and worry.

Think about sending your child to a Kumon School for additional help. Tim Smith felt they were old fashioned in a good way. The Kumon Method consists of page after page of carefully structured questions that slowly become more difficult each time. The kids are given a sheet where they have to get twenty out of twenty, and then, and only then, can they move onto to the next concept. The Kumon Method is completely based on traditional rote learning and drill. http://www.kumon.co.uk/

### How do I make my child's ropey teachers better?

So you've noticed that your child's book is never marked, that he seems bored by the work he is set or you're hearing nightmare stories about the class running riot during lessons. What do you do?

Firstly, talk to the teacher. Don't believe everything you've heard either from your child or other parents. Talk to the poor, long-suffering teacher in a friendly fashion. He or she is probably teaching during the day so leave a message with the school office or email. When you speak to the teacher, make sure you focus on your child (as opposed to attacking their teaching methods) by asking the crucial questions: 'How much is he or she learning and what can be done to improve his or her work?'

All pupils are entitled now to an 'Individual Action Plan' (IAP) in subjects they are not doing well in; this is a clear plan of action about how improvements could be made with deadlines. A typical 'IAP' for a Year 8 English student who is bright but lazy might be:

1 Finish reading Philip Pullman's *Northern Lights* in three weeks time.
2 Write a review of *Northern Lights* using the framework set out by the teacher in four weeks.
3 Complete all other homework set in next few weeks.
4 Sit next to a pupil who will not distract during class
5 Show homework diary to parent every night.

Always keep the conversation constructive. Be nice! If there is ANYTHING that the teacher is doing right, praise him or her. They will love it and go the extra mile for your child.

**Do:**
Keep a paper trail. Keep notes/emails/letters. Make a note if you have had a bad experience with a teacher and date it. You may need it later on.
Thank the teacher for his hard work – even if he or she is a lazy sod! Get the teacher on your side.

Be tactful. Frame your complaint in positive language. Say what's going well and ask for suggestions about what might improve.

Set clear, time-bound targets.

**Don't:**
Get very angry or threaten.

Give up.

Be intimidated. You and your child have a lot of rights!

## When and how should you take complaints further?

If the teacher will not give your child an IAP or is persistently failing to 'meet his needs' as the jargon goes, you should take things a step further by writing to the headteacher about your concerns, and keeping a copy of any correspondence. From now on in, things are serious and you will need to retain evidence if you think you may have to really fight your corner.

If the headteacher does not resolve the problem, you should write to the governing body of the school with your complaint – your school will give you an outline of how to do this.

If that doesn't work, go to the next body in charge of the school: either the Local Authority or the Diocesan Body (for Roman Catholic and Church of England schools), or the relevant body – again your school will tell you what this is.

If that fails, you can write to the Secretary of State or the Children's Minister, outlining the sequence of events that has led you to complain to him or her. This really is a desperate last resort and may achieve little, except a lot of hoopla. Cynics might suggest contacting the press with your concerns to get some real action, explaining that you've written to the Secretary of State. Politicians are generally much more fearful of the media than anyone else. You could alternatively make a complaint to the school's inspectorate. Ofsted has the power to investigate a problem if: the school is not providing an adequate education; the pupils are underachieving or their needs are not being met; the school is poorly managed, or is not using its resources efficiently; the pupils' personal development and well-being are being neglected. However, these last measures are fairly drastic ones which shouldn't be necessary. One would hope that the governing body, if not the head teacher, will have been able to resolve the matter before it comes to this.

**Do:**
Be persistent.

Be polite.

Keep a paper trail: keep copies of emails/letters. Make notes about any meetings you have had.

**Don't:**
Be discouraged. What you are doing is very important: it may well help raise standards in the whole school.

Useful link: http://www.direct.gov.uk/en/Parents/Schoolslearn inganddevelopment/YourChildsWelfareAtSchool/ DG_4016106

## How could mentoring help my child do better?
Of all my pupils, Carly Springham, 17, isn't the sort you'd think would need mentoring. She isn't the truculent kid who is languishing at the bottom of the class, chucking bits of paper at the teacher and yelling at anyone who annoys her. She's a quiet, hard-working student who's got good GCSEs, comes from a stable home background and is doing reasonably well in her second year in the sixth form at the large comprehensive school where I teach, in London's suburbs. However, she is adamant that mentoring has really helped her to improve her grades, her work and her attitude to her studies.

'Before I started going to see my learning mentor I was doing OK at my subjects, but I wasn't doing my best. I was coasting a bit, getting C grades when I should have been aiming for Bs and As,' she confessed to me. As her English teacher, I'd highlighted in her grades for effort that she wasn't trying as hard as she could, and this had led to her getting a learning mentor at my school.

The headteacher, David Mansfield, has recently hired learning mentors not because the school is stuffed full of underachieving layabouts – it isn't, it gains some of the best results in the country – but because recent government research has shown that mentoring can make average pupils exceptional.

'Parents shouldn't think that mentoring is simply for students who are at the bottom of the pile,' he told me. 'Mentoring can really help those pupils who are perhaps achieving B grades but who should be getting A*s. The reason why it works is that it is an excellent way of making a student more "accountable". The one-on-one attention students get when they are mentored means that they get to review their work in a non-threatening fashion, and then set clear, achievable targets to improve the situation.'

This is exactly how Carly's learning mentor, Samantha King, is with her students: unremittingly positive. 'I see my role as breaking down the barriers between pupils and teachers. I never punish my mentees; I listen to them, absorb as much as I can about their lives and set realistic targets, which I check up on every week,' she says.

'I love going to see Mrs King because she never tells me off!' Carly says. 'I can be honest and say what's going on in my life; tell her that I've been lazy or I've got other things on my mind, and she'll help me to devise a timetable that will get me out of a fix. She has really helped me to stop feeling overwhelmed by all the work I have to do for my A-levels.' Carly's life, like many teenagers, is also full of other distractions: she works ten hours a week in a shoe shop, takes driving lessons, socialises with friends, shops for clothes, and chats at length on MSN.

And, while they might be doing pretty well, they are very often not fulfilling their true potential because of poor time-management skills. As a result, these pupils, particularly high-achieving girls, tend to work in a blind panic and, despite producing satisfactory work, end up hating the process. A good mentor can bring the enjoyment back to school work simply by guiding a pupil to organise their life better.

Many mentors come from backgrounds outside teaching, which means they bring a fresh perspective for many pupils. Samantha King, who has worked in the corporate world for many years, naturally commands the pupils' respect because she is able to show how crucial time-management is to any decent job. She says: 'Mentoring for teenagers involves quite a bit of general careers advice. For example, I've mentored some pupils who are working in paid employment for many hours each week and I've explained to them that, although they may be getting good money now, in the long run they'll miss out if they don't get a good degree.'

Some schools have gone one step farther and arranged for their pupils to have professional mentors – this is when a pupil is hooked up with a successful professional in a job that the teenager aspires to. The charity African and Caribbean Diversity (www.acdiversity.org), which assists inner-city children from African and Caribbean backgrounds, has developed a hugely successful programme of professional mentoring, where bright pupils from inner-city London schools are mentored by high-flyers.

One such luminary is Peter Jaffe, the executive director in risk at the investment bank JP Morgan, who has been the mentor of Jordan Douglas White, an A-level student at Kingsbury High School, in South London, for the past two years. The experience has been rewarding for both of them. Thanks in part to his mentoring, Jordan achieved top grades in his GCSEs and is on track to study computer science at a leading university.

Jaffe says: 'Jordan and I took part in what is known as professional team mentoring. This is where a pupil is "shared" between two mentors, and each mentor sees Jordan once a month. The scheme is co-ordinated by ACD but involves the school and parents as much as possible. It enabled Jordan to get a different perspective, in the real world of work. And I found it a rewarding experience: I am now definitely plugged into the younger generation.'

The benefits for Jordan have been enormous: he has gone to museums and galleries with his mentor, as well as being able to talk about all the key issues in his life, his ambitions and the way he organises his time. He says: 'I tend to slack off slightly, but my mentor has been able to tell me about organising my time in a much better way. I won £50 for a presentation I gave on selling a laptop. I think having a mentor has really improved my confidence.'

It's a win-win situation for everyone involved. The corporate institutions involved realise that they need to be in touch with the talent of tomorrow and to foster their enthusiasm and skill, while the students gain a significant insight into the high-powered workplace.

Unfortunately, it is not always possible to line up a good adult mentor for pupils who are underachieving. One way round this is to set up peer mentoring programmes, where an older pupil mentors a younger one within strict parameters. Having trialled it in my own school, this can be tremendously successful. In my role as head of English in a large comprehensive, I arranged for a number of slack 16-year-old students to be assigned sixth-form mentors to help them with their English.

My instructions to mentors and students were clear and precise: they were to meet twice a week in their own time for 10-20 minutes and discuss the set texts on the syllabus. I was very pleasantly surprised when some of my naughtiest students began to rave about it. One previously surly teenager enthused to me: 'Sir, I met my mentor today and I think I understand Thomas Hardy for the first time in my life!' The exercise does require essential preparation from the teacher, but if everyone is fully committed, mentoring can transform children's futures, no matter what their background.

For more information, including details about how to search for a mentor: http://www.mentoring-uk.org.uk

# Hea*l*th

*If you want children to keep their feet on the ground,*
*put some responsibility on their shoulders.* **Abigail Van Buren**

**Making Sure Your Child is Safe, Healthy and Happy at School**
The government has placed these issues absolutely at the heart of what they do in schools in the coming years. The need for change was made apparent in Lord Laming's report into the death of Victoria Climbié, the young girl who was horrifically abused and tortured, and eventually killed by her great-aunt and the man with whom they lived. In the view of Laming, some schools were not looking at the 'whole child', not considering children's well-being much beyond their academic achievements. This led to a re-assessment of what should be demanded from schools.

The new guidance and regulation for schools aims to make sure that children will:

- Be healthy
- Stay safe

- Enjoy and achieve
- Make a positive contribution
- Achieve economic well-being

What does this actually mean for your child? Well, the promises are very ambitious and quite hard-headed as well. They are worth knowing about because if your child's school is failing to address them, then they could be held accountable. Ofsted and the newly established Children's Commissioner are obliged to report upon them. Each area has a number of aims. These are:

| Outcomes | Aims | What this means for you and your child |
|---|---|---|
| Be healthy | Schools should do their best to ensure their pupils are:<br>• Physically healthy<br>• Mentally and emotionally healthy<br>• Sexually healthy<br>• Leading healthy lifestyles<br>• Choosing not to take illegal drugs | That there is decent sex and drugs education – where the facts and details are explained clearly.<br><br>Good school dinners, lots of PE, swimming, dancing, gymnastics, competitive games should be on the curriculum. |
| Stay safe | Schools should do their best to ensure their pupils are:<br>• Safe from maltreatment, neglect, violence and sexual exploitation<br>• Safe from accidental injury and death<br>• Safe from bullying and discrimination<br>• Safe from crime and anti-social behaviour in and out of school<br>• Secure, stable and are cared for | Dealing with any bullying promptly and effectively.<br><br>Eradicating yobbery from schools and the local area.<br><br>Providing good health and safety. |

| Outcomes | Aims | What this means for you and your child |
|---|---|---|
| Enjoy and achieve | Schools should do their best to ensure their pupils:<br>• Have the right equipment – books etc – for school<br>• Attend and enjoy school<br>• Achieve stretching national educational standards at primary school<br>• Achieve personal and social development and enjoy recreation<br>• Achieve stretching national educational standards at secondary school | Your child should like school!<br><br>They should get Level 4s or above in Key Stage 2 tests and 5 A*-C grades at GCSE including English, maths and science |
| Make a positive contribution | Schools should do their best to ensure their pupils:<br>• Engage in decision making and support the community and environment<br>• Engage in law-abiding and positive behaviour in and out of school<br>• Develop positive relationships and choose not to bully and discriminate<br>• Develop self-confidence and successfully deal with significant life changes and challenges<br>• Develop enterprising behaviour | Be involved in local decision making<br><br>Be involved with discussing and deciding what kind of education you and your child want |
| Achieve economic well-being | Schools should do their best to ensure their pupils:<br>• Engage in further education, employment or training on leaving school<br>• Are ready for employment<br>• Live in decent homes and sustainable communities<br>• Have access to transport and material goods<br>• Live in households free from low income | Go to university/get properly qualified<br>Get a good job<br>Live in a decent home |

These outcomes and aims have led to some specific targets that were outlined in the Children's Plan in December 2007:

- At age 5, 90% of children will be developing well across all areas of the early years foundation stages
- At age 11, 95% of children will have reached expected levels in literacy and numeracy
- At age 16, 90% will have achieved the equivalent of five good GCSEs
- At age 18, the majority of children will be ready for higher education with at least 6 out of 10 children achieving the equivalent of A-levels
- Child poverty will be halved by 2010 and eradicated by 2020
- There will be clear improvements in child health, with the proportion of overweight children reduced to 2000 levels
- The number of first time young offenders will be reduced so that by 2020 the number receiving a conviction, reprimand or final warning for a recordable offence has fallen by a quarter.

For more information:
http://www.everychildmatters.gov.uk/information/

**Food and Diet**

In terms of ensuring that your child has a healthy diet, much can be done at home, through example and discussion, to make sure they are aware of what constitutes healthy eating.

**Do:**

Grow food in your back garden or on the window sill. Get your child in touch with where food comes from.

Cook fresh food with your child. Involve them as much as possible.

Discuss the issues with your child, and find out what they know about the content of the junk food they are eating.

Establish a routine of healthy eating. Draw up a time-table for the week using the charts outlined below to help you.

**Don't:**
Ban junk food entirely. Keep it as a treat.

For more guidance, see :
http://www.schoolfoodtrust.org.uk

**What do I do if my child has food allergies?**
The school is obliged to help manage this situation. Many schools are finding that cases of peanut, milk, egg and other allergies are on the increase. The Anaphylaxis campaign states that even the most extreme form of allergy – anaphylaxis – should not be ignored by your child's school: they need to help. You should think about cross contamination when considering their child's lunch and how this can be significantly lowered by washing hands with soap after handling or eating nuts.

See your GP or/and http://www.allergyinschools.co.uk

**What about packed lunches?**
Watch out! The food fascists are about. Teachers are allowed to inspect packed lunches and recommend that they do not include:

- Sugary or sweetened soft drinks
- Sweets
- Chocolate or items covered in chocolate
- Crisps
- Cereal bars

But they are not allowed to confiscate them!

## How do I stop my child getting fat?

One in three children will be obese by 2010 according to the Department of Health so this is clearly a problem. The best ways to prevent children becoming overweight are:

- Walk to school, walk to the shops, walk to as many places as you can!
- Involve your child in your food shopping, making them aware of the healthy choices.
- Avoid giving them unhealthy snacks, if they are hungry between meals insist they eat fruit or healthier snacks.
- Give your school a hard time if they are not meeting the new food standards; tell the governors, the headteacher.

For more information: http://www.eatwell.gov.uk
http://www.schoolfoodtrust.org.uk


## How do I keep my child safe and healthy at school?

I've sat upon the 'Health and Safety' committee at my school for a number of years now and I think I can safely say that there are some lessons and places in school where problems hardly ever occur – and places where they do quite a bit. The danger areas are all predictable: the science labs, design and technology lessons when equipment like hammers, nails and drills are being used, PE lessons with activities like trampolining, high jump, rugby.

There is a huge mass of legislation about school health and safety; all schools are now obliged to make sure that pupils don't get electrocuted by faulty plugs or drowned in the school pond. The biggest problem you'll face is that society's obsession with health and safety means that there is much less fun stuff going on in school because it's deemed to be too risky. Most science teachers prefer to show pupils videos of experiments rather than do them in class, most drama teachers stick on a DVD rather than go to the theatre, most history teachers read through a text book rather than re-enacting the Battle of Hastings; in the vast majority of cases, it's health and safety to blame!

Interestingly, the government is concerned about this and have set up something called the Council for Learning Outside the Classroom (www.lotc.org.uk). If you are concerned about the lack of opportunities for your child to learn outside the class-room, it's well worth looking at its website before you go stomp-ing off to the headteacher to complain; the website provides some constructive ways of addressing the issue, although it remains to be seen whether it's yet another toothless quango chewing up public money uselessly.

If you are concerned about any aspect of health and safety, you should find out who is responsible for it in a school; this var-ies depending upon what type of school it is. If in doubt, contact the headteacher's PA and find out! Most health and safety officers I've come across are eminently sensible people who don't want to stop enjoyable activities. Nevertheless, they are in a position to carry out risk assessments if they are concerned that an activ-ity may be dangerous. If you are worried about an activity, you should request a risk assessment. Once that's been carried out, the Health and Safety officer will be in a position to judge what to do next: whether the activity needs to be made safer, stopped or can carry on as it is.

**Do:**

Encourage your child to take part in outdoor activities.

Encourage your school to run 'riskier' experiments.

Ask for a risk assessment if you are worried about the safety of an activity.

Check out these websites for more information: Council for Learning Outside the Classroom http://www.lotc.org.uk

http://www.direct.gov.uk/en/Parents/Schoolslearninganddevelopment/YourChildsWelfareAtSchool/

**Don't:**
Suffer in silence. Contact the health and safety officer if you are worried.

**Who is the person who protects my child from abuse?**
Every school has a Child Protection Officer. If you are worried your child is being abused by a member of staff or pupil, you must report it immediately to the Child Protection Officer in the first instance; your school will tell you who this is. They have a legal duty to report it to the relevant authorities and are trained to deal with it.

**CASE STUDY The weird PE teacher**
Gillian had been hearing some strange stories about her son's PE teacher for a while. Tales told more in amusement than anything else after nearly every lesson he took. Firstly, there was his obsession with making the children stand in straight lines. Apparently, he would go ballistic if any kid did not stand absolutely straight and still, keeping rigidly to the line. Her son, George, had been shouted at a number of times because he had failed to assume the correct posture. The PE teacher, Mr W, would put his face right up to anyone who he didn't like and yell at them with the full force of his tonsils. Although George laughed about it, Gillian could tell it was an unnerving and unpleasant experience – and a reaction that was completely over-the-top considering the 'crime'. However, Gillian became more disturbed when she heard that Mr W would gather up any clothes that were left lying around in a messy fashion in the changing rooms. This meant that children would return from their showers to find their clothes had gone. They would then

have to go to Mr W, who was standing outside the changing rooms, in only their towels to get their clothes back. On one occasion, Mr W had sneered at what he felt was George's 'puny body'.

Gillian didn't want to cause a fuss: she was aware that she didn't really have any hard evidence. However, she decided to report Mr W's behaviour to the headteacher. A few weeks later, Mr W was suspended for inappropriate behaviour. Apparently, his behaviour towards a few of the boys in the football team had been worse – much worse. But nothing had been said for years because, despite being very odd, Mr W was a popular teacher: he devoted himself to the school's sports' teams and got excellent results. A trial ensued and Mr W was found guilty of sexually abusing a young boy in his care.

Gillian won't know if her initial complaint led to a more serious investigation but she feels relieved she did voice her concerns. 'My advice is: if you feel uneasy about something, always report it,' she says.

For more information:
http://www.parentscentre.gov.uk/educationandlearning/school life/healthandwelfare/childprotection/

**Do:**
Contact the Child Protection officer immediately if you are concerned about a teacher or a pupil being abusive.

Make sure a careful investigation is carried out.

Contact the police if you are very concerned.

**Don't:**
Spread malicious rumours without any evidence.

Suffer in silence.

**What do I do if I think my child has mental health problems?**

A recent UNICEF report highlighted the fact that Britain has the unhappiest children in Europe. A toxic mix of pressure at school, the influence of the media, our materialistic culture, the easy availability of drugs and alcohol as well as a lack of parental involvement has meant that many children in the UK are effectively depressed.

What is good is that the stigma attached to mental health problems is beginning to be lifted. I come from a generation that almost universally despised people who had mental health issues. They were 'nutters', 'loonies', 'psychos'. Now both teachers and health professionals are beginning to realise that the most common health issues young people have to deal with are primarily 'mental'.

In 2004, the Office of National Statistics uncovered that one in ten children, aged 5–16 years, had a clinically diagnosed mental disorder. Four per cent had depression and six per cent had some kind of conduct disorder, which meant that there were severe problems with their behaviour. More recent research suggests that boys are twice as likely to have mental disorders than girls and that children from lone parent families were much more likely to have mental health issues. On the whole, the problem predominantly afflicts children from deprived backgrounds, in households where there are significant money worries, lots of siblings or low income.

That said, mental health problems afflict children from all social backgrounds. Some of the worst mental health problems I've seen have been with children from very aspirational middle-class homes who have felt that they have 'failed': failed to get the highest grades, failed to be the greatest sportsperson, failed to shine, failed to have a great body. In one extreme case, I know of one teenager who committed suicide because he did not get into Cambridge University.

Mental health issues may not be obvious but warning signs could be:

- Your child stops talking to you
- Has sleepless nights, is wetting the bed
- Doesn't want to go to school
- Isn't motivated by important things such as seeing friends, doing work they usually enjoy
- Seems listless and lacking in energy
- Feels ill much of the time but with no obvious physical signs of illness.

**Do:**

Investigate the issue thoroughly. Look around your child's room, keep a close eye on him/her at home.

Think about why your child might be depressed. For example, if you and your partner are having lots of rows, this could be a catalyst.

Be positive and upbeat. Look at the positives in your child's life. Praise him/her.

Try and talk things through with your child. Ask them about how they are feeling and whether they have anything on their mind.

Talk to someone if you are worried about your child. Your GP, a helpline (listed below), a school counsellor or your child's tutor/year head.

**Don't:**

Panic. This will only make the situation worse.

Feel alone. This problem is much more common than you would think. Get in touch with a support network if necessary.

Get angry with your child.

Label your child as a pest, an idiot etc.

Tell them they are 'nutty', 'stupid', 'psycho'.

**Helpful numbers/contacts:**
Young Minds on 0800 018 2138 – a parents' information service providing confidential advice for any adult concerned about the mental health or emotional well-being of a child or young person. http://www.youngminds.org.uk/

Parentline Plus helpline on 0808 800 2222 – provides help and information for anyone caring for children. http://www. parentlineplus.org.uk/

Child Line on 0800 1111 – offers help to young people in trouble or danger. http://www.childline.org.uk/Pages/default. aspx

**Helping your child develop the stamina to survive state school**
One of the biggest problems that your child faces at school may not be extreme; they might not be the victim of extreme bullying, nightmarishly incompetent teaching or suffer from Special Educational Needs. It might be just that the process of being at school exhausts them. State schools tend to be big, bustling, noisy places, full of children and teachers shouting, eating, laughing and joking. Many of them are the exact opposite of peaceful sanctuaries of calm and studious quiet. One of the reasons why many parents send their children to private schools is because they want to give their child a 'smaller stage' on which to develop at their own pace. The larger state institutions do not always feel as friendly and cosy as the smaller private schools: they can, with their high fences, long, maze-like corridors and numerous classrooms, feel very impersonal.

In this environment, the unassuming, shy, quiet child can find too much of their time is taken up with being pushed to the back of the dinner queue, keeping up with banter, trying to keep a low profile because they're the 'red-headed' one, or the 'fat' one, or the 'speccy' one.

One of the most important qualities to help your child develop in this context is stamina, both mental and physical. To do this, you'll need to discuss it with your child and think of 'stamina' strategies.

This might include:

• Having a bigger breakfast, eating porridge etc – energy levels during the day are closely related to the amount of breakfast a child has. Carrying around snacks such as fruit and nuts and bananas which give energy can also help.

• Learning to distract attention away from trouble by telling jokes and not taking things too seriously. But be wary of them turning into the class clown as a survival technique, there is a balance...

• Finding places of 'sanctuary' in a school such as the library (or 'learning resources centre' as it is now known in many schools!) or by joining clubs.

• Finding a buddy who is sympathetic.

# Beha*vio*ur

*What's done to children, they will do to society.*
**Karl Menninger**

### What do I do if my child misbehaves at school?

Firstly, you're going to need to work out what the school considers to be bad behaviour. Having taught in many different schools, I know this can vary hugely. For example, at a Catholic girls' school where I taught for a few years, girls could get excluded for smoking in their uniform outside school or being rude to shopkeepers and bus drivers. In other schools I've worked in, these would have been considered to be laughably minor offences and pupils would have been let off with a reprimand at worst.

Still, it's worth looking carefully at the relevant policies that the school have drawn up. Legally, all schools must have a clear discipline policy, which is drawn up by the headteacher. The best schools will have a clear policy which all the pupils and staff KNOW about, and ENFORCE it. Expectations about behaviour and sanctions against bad behaviour will be very clear. Above all, there will be a clear series of sanctions such as:

- A reprimand
- A letter home
- Removal from a class or group
- Loss of privileges
- Confiscating something belonging to your child if it's inappropriate for school (for example, a mobile phone or music player)
- Detention

These sanctions should walk hand-in-hand with a clear system of rewards, such as commendations for good behaviour, prizes for good work, and privileges for those who are responsible and help out.

The best schools give their pupils positions of responsibility and these are their ultimate reward.

**Do:**
Raise your concerns about any misbehaviour with the headteacher or your Parent Governor.

Discuss your worries and anxieties with your child.

Discuss the reasons why misbehaviour happens.

Try and address the root causes of the misbehaviour.

Give your child some strategies to help them behave.

Be positive with your child. Praise them when they behave well.

Play games with your child.

Ignore minor misbehaviour.

**Don't:**
Get angry and shout abuse/insults at your child.

Hit your child.

Punish them.

### Do detentions really work?

The 1997 Education Act gives schools the right to detain pupils if they give parents 24 hours notice. So you can't really argue with them, even if you think your child has been given one unfairly; the school has a legal right to detain a child.

In my experience as a teacher, detentions work best when one or two pupils are made an example of and clobbered hard with a long detention if they are misbehaving. The Renaissance philosopher, Machiavelli, suggested in his handbook for rulers, *The Prince*, that punishments need to meted out swiftly and act as a deterrent to others. This is certainly true with teaching: the times when I've bunged some miscreants into detention at the first sign of trouble have been productive. The rest of the class have seen that I mean business and have bucked up and behaved. So I feel parents should be supportive of teachers who do this. However, problems can start when teachers resort to holding a class back in detention repeatedly, week after week, month after month; a negative cycle begins and the relationship between teacher and pupil breaks down. Then parents need to question what is going on, taking up the matter with the teacher and their line manager.

### When can a teacher use reasonable force?

This is a big and thorny question; teachers are, contrary to what you might read in the press, allowed to use 'reasonable force' with a pupil if they think he or she might self-harm, injure someone else, damage property or cause serious disruption. They can also search pupils for offensive weapons such as knives.

## CASE STUDY   Are these powers enough?

Tony, a little boy in an oversized uniform, was trembling at the back of the playground. As I approached I could see why. He had fresh bruises on his face and little knife cuts on the back of his hand. At the far corner of the playground, I saw John, a large boy of 13 hovering, watching Tony and me closely. I asked Tony whether he was being picked on. His arm looked like someone had cut him with a knife. With a look of anxiety on his face, Tony denied this.

Wondering why John was hovering so circumspectly, I asked to look in his bag. He refused point-blank. I retreated, knowing that I didn't have the power to do anything. I decided to fill in a report to Tony's year head instead, voicing my suspicions. It was all I could do in the circumstances. A couple of hours later, John's father phoned to complain that I had been wanting to look through his 'private possessions'.

Thankfully, new powers granted in 2007 give teachers like me the legal right to search pupils if we suspect they may have a weapon. Characters like John will no longer be able to bully kids with knives and get away with it, and parents like John's father will no longer be able to complain. I know I will be joined by many of my fellow teachers in applauding the government for having – for once – given us a little more power to impose order in our chaotic secondary schools.

The statistics show that many schools are lawless places. A recent report by the schools' inspectorate revealed declining standards of behaviour in secondary schools – a third of lessons are disrupted by poor behaviour.

Last year the police had to be called a number of times to avert riots at my local secondary school; one parent told me that her 15-year-old son had admitted to carrying a knife to school for self-defence. She, and many other parents like her throughout the country, are now grateful that the school has the power to search pupils thoroughly – with metal detectors – before they enter the premises. Eventually, the school will become a safer place.

But how did we get to this sorry state, where schools have to waste precious resources and time on checking that pupils are not carrying weapons? Ironically, the law has undoubtedly played a big role in the breakdown of order. For example, we are not legally allowed to detain a pupil for more than 20 minutes after school without giving 24 hours written notice to a pupil's parent. In particular, the Human Rights Act means that children can still sue or sack teachers if they feel their 'privacy, dignity and physical integrity' has been compromised. One colleague of mine was suspended for a year while an allegation that he had hit a child while stopping a fight was investigated – it was eventually proved to be false. Often headteachers and governing bodies take the side of the pupils if there are a number of pupils saying that the teacher is in the wrong. The result? Many teachers would simply rather not get involved. You're far better off letting the pupils beat the hell out of each other than intervening.

Much of the time the teacher is not, however, the target of disruption: it's bullying and squabbling among a peer group that causes the worst problems, because disagreements can rumble on for weeks, months, years, erupting without warning in classrooms and playgrounds. The internet and mobile phones have aggravated the situation: now a nasty rumour, an embarrassing photo, a cutting remark can be spread around and within seconds everyone knows about it. In this climate, pupils seek revenge. Many teenagers have been murdered in London recently, essentially over very trivial remarks: it appeared that they 'dissed' or disrespected the wrong people.

The truth is that in large schools, teachers are overwhelmed. Pupil behaviour is much better in primary schools. This isn't simply because the children are younger, it's also because the schools are smaller and teachers are better able to form proper relationships with their pupils. A survey in April 2007 showed that temporary exclusions are running at nearly 10 per cent of pupils in secondary schools – that's schools with more than 1,000 pupils – compared with three per cent in those with 1,000 or fewer children. We need to look at ways of making schools more manageable in size. Simply giving teachers the legal right to search pupils for weapons isn't enough. Ultimately, we need to break up our larger schools into smaller units.

**What might happen if my child is very badly behaved?**
Exclusions are a school's ultimate – and some would say – only serious sanction: their last resort for dealing with seriously bad behaviour. There are two types of exclusion: fixed-term (which are temporary) and permanent. As with everything in the state sector, there are numerous guidelines and laws relating to exclusions. In order to get excluded, your child needs to be VERY BADLY BEHAVED!

Typical reasons for fixed-term exclusions are:

- Fighting other pupils
- Extreme rudeness to a teacher such as
  telling him or her to 'fuck off'
- Persistently disrupting lessons
- Stealing
- Smoking or taking drugs in school

Only a headteacher or acting headteacher can exclude a pupil and a child can't be given fixed period (non-permanent) exclusions which total more than 45 school days in any one school year. If the exclusion is longer than a day, work must be set and marked. Parents should also be sent a letter which explains clearly the reasons for the exclusion and sets out what a parent's duties are during the time of the exclusion.

The main thing to bear in mind is that there is huge variation between schools about when and why pupils are excluded. Some headteachers have been known to exclude 200 pupils in one day for relatively trivial offences in order to set an example, other headteachers hardly exclude at all.

Personally, I am not convinced exclusions work. In most cases, pupils I have taught who have been given fixed-term exclusions have nearly always come back in a much more aggressive and disaffected state – see the case studies below. Some schools exclude 'internally'; that is pupils are put in 'isolation rooms' where they supposedly get on with work. Again, I am suspicious of such rooms; it is rare that any learning goes on there. I would be very wary if you learn that your child has been 'internally excluded'; no figures are kept on this type of exclusion and frequently pupils are left to rot.

The best schools have real systems for supporting pupils who have behavioural problems or are not learning properly in the normal classroom; they'll employ mentors to work one-to-one with pupils, put pupils in smaller classes, give them extra help with their basic skills and work with parents to find ways of getting them to improve their attitude.

If things have really broken down and the headteacher feels that a pupil can't function properly in a school because their behaviour is totally unacceptable, then 'permanent exclusion' becomes the option; most permanent exclusions are handed out for persistently disruptive behaviour, but sometimes, in extreme cases, pupils have been expelled for a one-off offence such as hitting a teacher. In most cases though, headteachers need to have a very long and painstaking paper trail if they are going to permanently exclude a pupil: they need to show their governing body through hard, documented evidence that everything has been done to prevent a pupil from misbehaving. If a governing body feels that there is insufficient evidence to back up the school's case against a pupil, it can overturn a headteacher's decision to exclude permanently. Parents can also appeal against the exclusion by going to an independent appeal panel, organised by the Local Authority, who will listen to the case.

My advice to parents in this position is to appeal! Pupils who are permanently excluded are ten times more likely to wind up in prison and to fail to enter the education system again. If there is any chance your child can stay in the school, then go for it. Most children need stability, particularly children under the threat of exclusion. The overwhelming majority of them come from poor, deprived backgrounds and have learning difficulties. Permanent exclusion doesn't help them at all; it just sets them firmly on the path to failure, and potentially criminality.

While your child may never be excluded, it's important for you and him or her to understand the deep-rooted reasons why pupils are sometimes kicked out. Put simply: it very often starts at home. It doesn't take a rocket scientist to work out that if a child has grown up in a turbulent, unsupportive home, they bring those issues into school with them. The best schools can deal with these children if there are properly trained teachers around and decent support systems. Unfortunately, not enough funding has been put into this area and schools can really struggle.

## CASE STUDIES Excluded children: what every parent should know about exclusions

Mohammed was only 13 years old and wasn't especially tall or powerful, yet I was terrified of him. 'I'll fucking kill you. Do you get what I mean, geezer? I'll fucking deck you!' he screamed at me as I asked him to leave my classroom. He had hit a boy over the head and spent much of the lesson swearing. By this time, I was trembling with rage and fear, and was relieved when he finally left the room.

Soon afterwards Mohammed was excluded from the school and I decided to take a break from teaching. It was 1997 and the chaos he had caused had sapped my confidence. Because the school was not a stereotypical inner-city comprehensive, but located in a prosperous London suburb, I felt doubly deflated; I felt that I had become horribly soft. In fact, the school did have significant problems with discipline, with a considerable rump of children from troubled backgrounds, but few teachers there were trained to cope with the more challenging pupils such as Mohammed. Rowdy classes became riotous, lessons became war zones. Many of the parents were in the dark over this because the school had a good reputation and handled its PR with parents well.

Several years later, with my spirits refreshed and missing the buzz and excitement of the classroom, I returned to full-time teaching, quickly becoming a head of department at a school in Havering, outer London. In this new position of responsibility, I had to teach several children who had been excluded from other schools or who had been passed on to me by more junior teachers. By this time, I had become a more tolerant teacher, less obsessed with results, more adept at handling disruption. I was calmer and more consistent in my approach. Some of my pupils were potentially just as aggressive as Mohammed had been, but I was able to cope with them; I'd learned to 'give and take', to negotiate, to form good relationships with difficult children.

One child, John, had been permanently excluded from another school but had settled in well at my new school and ultimately succeeded in attaining eight good GCSEs. I recently spoke to him about how his life had progressed and was delighted to hear that everything was going well for him. He had trained to be an electrician and was set, he said, on earning better wages than me. 'What I liked about the new school,' he told me, 'was that my mates and some of the teachers taught me how to deal with my anger. Sometimes I used to get so mad, I would just punch anyone who was around me, but then I learned to walk away from rucks. And I think that helped me concentrate more. The school stuck with me even though I was out of order sometimes. They didn't kick me out. That counts for a lot.'

Talking to John, I began to think about Mohammed, who had been jailed soon after being permanently excluded from school. I recalled how there were times when he had been keen on learning, had even shown interest in Shakespeare and reading. He had wanted to succeed, but I, and many other teachers at the school, had been preoccupied only by what was wrong with him, meting out punishments and threats that had caused a vicious spiral in his behaviour. During my investigations in trying to find out what had happened to him, I learned from another former pupil at the school that Mohammed was still 'up to no good'; he had become a drug dealer and had cut some heroin with washing powder and nearly killed a user.

Had I contributed to Mohammed's troubles? Had my old school failed him? If extra resources had been available to give him proper care and attention, would we have spared society huge amounts of money and distress in the long term?

Mohammed fitted the typical profile of an excluded child. He was male, of mixed race, had special educational needs and was in foster care. He was permanently excluded in 1997, exactly at the point when the new Labour administration swept to power promising to address the problems presented by children like him. Tony Blair's mantra, 'Education, education, education', was as much about clamping down on the Mohammeds of this world, about being 'tough on the causes of crime', as it was about improving results.

In spite of the government's best efforts to massage the figures, exclusion rates have remained more or less the same for a decade; on average, roughly 9,000 children or more are permanently excluded from school every year and nearly 400,000 children given 'fixed-term' exclusions, according to the Department for Children, Schools and Families. Eighty per cent of them are boys. Government figures show that Roma children are three and a half times more likely to be excluded than other children, and those from black or mixed ethnic backgrounds are twice as likely to be excluded as whites. Children in care are eight times as likely to be excluded, and those with special educational needs are three times more likely to be ordered to leave their school.

After 12 years of a Labour government, school exclusions continue to affect the underprivileged. In 2007, as many as 140,000 pupils who were excluded for short periods from school were eligible for free meals, accounting for a third of such exclusions, even though these children make up only 12 per cent of the school population.

Meanwhile, society as a whole is paying an increasing cost. Significant research by the charity New Philanthropy Capital reveals that the average excluded child costs society more than £63,851 a year. This figure includes the future lost earnings of the child resulting from poor qualifications, and also costs to society in terms of crime, health and social services. In total, this amounts to £650m a year. This is probably a gross underestimate, since many excluded children are not accounted for in the figures.

What many parents – and teachers – don't realise is that the human cost of failing to deal with the problem is incalculable: 50 per cent of men in prison were excluded from school. 'Research shows that at the root of school exclusions, and much crime, is the inability of young people to communicate properly,' says Lord Ramsbotham, former chief inspector of prisons. 'If we addressed these problems in the classroom, many of our problems with antisocial behaviour would disappear. At the moment, what happens is that these young people, having been alienated from their families at an early age, are then excluded from school and turn to crime: drug-taking and dealing, knife crime and, in extreme but increasing cases, murder. Research shows that while poor parenting and low socio-economic status are major factors, school exclusion plays a significant environmental role in helping shape the criminals of tomorrow. The government needs to appoint a minister for inclusion to begin to address these issues.'

Ofsted, in its report, *Reducing Exclusions of Black Pupils from Secondary Schools: Examples of Good Practice,* identified three interrelated features that significantly reduce exclusions: 'Respect for the individual in school and a systematic, caring and consistent approach to behaviour and personal development, the courage and willingness to discuss difficult issues, a focus on helping pupils to take more control of their lives by providing them with strategies to communicate well and look after each other.'

I know from my own experience that good mentoring really helps; the best schools allocate both 'academic' and 'professional' mentors to troubled pupils. The academic mentor will set clear, achievable targets twice a week which are then closely monitored, while professional mentors, usually drawn from the world of work, will show pupils opportunities beyond the classroom.

Frequently, these pupils have tailor-made numeracy and literacy lessons, and work in small groups with tutors to engage with the curriculum. Furthermore, pupils with particular psychological needs will have relevant lessons such as 'anger management' classes or counselling sessions. While this may sound expensive, it needn't be: some schools have met the costs easily by getting rid of expensive management posts and reallocating the resources into buying in mentors and academic tutors.

Studies show that targeted early intervention can significantly reduce the problems caused by exclusions. Tim Walker, the chief executive at National Teaching & Advisory Service which assigns trained professionals to supervise the academic and social needs of excluded children says: 'Organisations like mine can make a big difference if we intervene at the right point; we can put troubled children on the path to success.'

The media is partly responsible for the situation too: for all the column inches devoted to antisocial behaviour and crime perpetrated by children, there is seldom any serious attempt to look at some of the mundane root causes. Pointing out the inconsistency in schools' approaches towards exclusions and the need for proper, uniform disciplinary procedures, doesn't make good copy. Screaming about the need to expel thugs and yobs from school does. As a result, the public is never properly informed about the issues and the debate remains banal.

There are straightforward, effective and cheap measures that could drastically reduce school exclusions tomorrow. But the political and educational will to implement them doesn't exist. And so we are condemning our society to an ever rising tide of lawlessness.

**Do:**

Remember that exclusions disproportionately affect children who come from deprived backgrounds and have special needs.

Get involved if you are concerned about misbehaviour in your child's school: talk to the headteacher about how you can help, become a mentor to a child.

Remember punishing these children usually doesn't work because they've seen far worse at home: they'll have been hit and beaten.

Don't be frightened of a difficult child. Say hello to them. Become their friend! Listen to them.

Be aware that overwhelmingly exclusions don't work for the excluded child.

Advocate the power of rehabilitation.

**Don't:**

Be ill-informed and ignorant and pass on your prejudices to your child. Try and talk through with your child the reasons why another child in their class may be disturbed: this is as much part of their education as academic lessons.

Make blanket demands for every troubled child to be chucked out.


## Would schools be better off if we brought back the cane?

In my second year of teaching at a tough inner city comprehensive in the early 1990s, I occasionally used to grab my insolent pupils by the arm and fling them out of the classroom – if they were small enough. Once or twice, I gave the really troublesome boys a light clip over the back of the head. Although corporal punishment was illegal by then, many other teachers there, still not fully cognisant with the law, did the same and far worse; once I saw a teacher grab and kick a pupil when he was lying on the ground. Nothing was done; it was all swept under the carpet. In the absence of any proper management to enforce strict discipline, chaos ruled in the school except in the classrooms where teachers were really macho and hard. What we weren't aware of was that the very machismo behaviour that temporarily made pupils behave was, in fact, leading to far worse problems throughout the school; it sanctioned all sorts of violent behaviour among the kids. If the teachers were biffing people, why couldn't they?

Desperate to keep some order in the classroom, I became a 'controloholic', addicted to controlling the behaviour of my pupils. I found that asking pupils to read in silence and threatening to chuck them out if they played up worked well; most of my classes in my second year were very well behaved, compared with the extremely unruly ones I had endured in my first year. However, looking back I am not sure that they learned much, except that they should obey. One of the major shortcomings of my lessons was that no discussion, group work or imaginative activities were permitted because that might open the way for chaos to ensue. In short, I wasn't teaching, I was child-minding in a particularly uninspiring fashion.

I came unstuck when I grabbed a pupil by the arms when he

disobeyed me, refusing to play Macbeth in a shortened version of the play. He ran out of the classroom and complained to the deputy head, who reprimanded me and warned me never to do it again. Which I haven't. That was more than 15 years ago and my attitudes towards corporal punishment have changed hugely since then. I no longer believe in it; I have seen firsthand that it just doesn't work. Once you feel you have sanctioned the use of violence, you cease thinking imaginatively, rationally and strategically about solving behavioural problems. Children cease to be people, merely robots to be re-programmed with a boot up the backside. Teaching stops being about relationships and all about obedience.

I am not surprised, though, that one in five teachers wants to bring back the cane. As I have seen myself, in countless classrooms during my decade and a half as a teacher in state schools, many British children are out of control, unwilling to listen, eager to answer back, and reluctant to work on anything that doesn't stimulate their interest immediately. Bringing back the cane seems like the only solution in the face of this desperate situation.

Of course, it isn't. Many of our worst behaved children live in violent households, where they are beaten regularly by their parents. Not surprisingly, angry and disaffected, they bring this violence into the classroom, seeking to solve their problems with their fists and abuse. These vulnerable, sad, defeated children need properly trained teachers to deal with them; I have seen myself that there are strategies that really work such as finding a curriculum that engages them, giving them proper counselling, helping them get motivated in a positive, 'emotionally intelligent' fashion. However, from being a refuge, frequently school is even more of a nightmare for these children; many of them can't read or write properly and more often than not they hate their lessons. The current system is very inflexible; school budgets are over-stretched and targeted support doesn't happen. In the cases when it does, such as when Save The Children's Ear To Listen project enables children to have an 'advocate' who mediates between home and school, bringing them the right help and guidance, the results are remarkable; the poor behaviour stops and they start to learn.

Bringing back the cane would be an unmitigated disaster for our schools; we need to use our intellect, not our fists, to make our children motivated to learn.

## The importance of routine

Many studies into the psychology of happiness have shown again and again that winning the lottery or receiving a windfall of money doesn't make people any happier in the long run if it disrupts the routines that made those people happy in the first place. In fact, some people become a great deal more miserable if what made them feel fulfilled in life is removed by the sudden arrival of millions. Effectively, this has happened to many people in the developed world. We are a much wealthier society than we used to be fifty years ago. The old routines such as washing our own clothes, doing the dishes, making our own food, walking to the shops and amusing ourselves in the evenings have been swept away and replaced by machines that can do all these things for us. There isn't the same necessity for a routine, and many of us are unhappier as a result. You can help introduce a happy and balanced routine into your child's life, which will give them security and a fulfilled day-to-day existence.

**Do:**
Establish clear times and places where work is done.

Establish a reasonable timetable of social activities: ration going out. Agree reasonable terms with your child.

Make your child see the intrinsic value of work but also help them see that some work is boring but it just has to be done. That's life!

Pay attention to them by having family meals together, reading stories to them before they go to bed.

**Don't:**
Leave your child alone with the internet for ages on end – put the computer in a communal area.


**British teenagers today**

Back in the mists of time, in the late 1980s, when I first started teaching, life was relatively uncomplicated for the British teenager. They had far less distractions and pressures than today. They might watch too much TV, play the odd badly animated computer game, hang around with their friends on street corners yearning for the latest designer shoes or have ambitions to buy a great car. The internet was a name known only to science geeks, email only for celebrated academics, chatting on MSN, putting profiles on MySpace, Facebook, Bebo completely unheard of, X-boxes, Playstations, Guitar Hero games totally unconceived; Ipods, mobile phones, video phones and SAT-NAVs were gadgets that even science fiction movies hadn't dreamt of.

Perhaps most significantly, there was a great deal less pressure on children to be spectacular successes at school. League tables were yet to be introduced and teachers like me were not under instructions to get top results from every pupil. Instead, there was vague rhetoric about helping a child achieve their 'full potential', but senior managers were not threatening to withhold teachers' pay rises if their results were not up to snuff. As a result, there was a fairly relaxed atmosphere in most British classrooms. On the whole, even in the roughest of schools bar a few, an amiable companionship existed between pupil and teacher. The top achievers were not garlanded with prizes, nor were the lazy and hopeless labelled as losers.

How different things are now! Your average British child spends hours every day on the internet, chatting with their friends on MSN, checking out the latest coolest clips on You-Tube, comparing fashions and causes on Facebook or Bebo, playing a whole host of computer games; downloading, usually illegally, the trendiest music and playing it on what they hope will be the most envied Ipod currently available; watching their favourite TV programmes, recorded on Sky Plus; and socialising with friends, going to parties arranged quickly, covertly and haphazardly by mobile phone and the internet, where they will probably drink far too much alcohol bought cheaply at the local supermarket.

Add to all these social pressures to conform and to have the latest gear, the intense demands to do well in their exams and the result is that our teenagers are far more unhappy than when I first started teaching.

As I have mentioned before, a recent UNICEF survey revealed that Britain has the unhappiest and most troubled children in Europe: they are more likely to be depressed, to suffer from low self-esteem, to drink alcohol and to have under-age sex than their European counterparts. The report states that there is a well-established link between family breakdown, educational failure, poor health and reduced life chances.

What I've observed as a teacher in various comprehensives over the past two decades is that boys and girls have become unhappier in different ways. Many teenage girls I have taught strive for perfection in so many spheres: to appear sexually alluring, to be top of the class, to be the most popular girl, and most insidiously to be part of the 'toughest' girl gang. Meanwhile, many boys are infected with the desire to have the greatest footballing knowledge and acumen, and to have the best 'stuff'. Britain has become much more materialistic and this is reflected in the conversations I overhear teenagers having in school: endless talk about what gear, what gadgets, what clothes, what computers and what TVs they've got. And if they're not discussing that – perhaps surprisingly – they're discussing their school work: their grades and the homework they have to do – or avoid doing.

It all amounts to pressure, pressure, pressure from all sides and makes me wonder whether we've forgotten to teach our children that most vital skill: how to live a fulfilled and meaningful life.

I would draw back from saying that it is the job of teachers to make our children 'happy'. But as some of the key adults that children come into contact with during their formative years, we should be doing our best to steer them in the right direction.

Modern teenagers are suffering. I think, because they are so desperate to seek happiness instantly: by binge drinking, by having brief sexual encounters, by swotting madly for an exam, by watching a clip on YouTube and believing themselves to be experts on the subject immediately. They are less and less willing to enjoy activities in themselves, to see their intrinsic worth, less and less able to countenance absorbing knowledge and life in a slow, level-headed fashion: it is the end result that entrances them, not the getting there. As a consequence, they are permanently unsatisfied, always looking over their shoulders for the next best thing, whether this is in the academic or social sphere.

Ironically, the educational pressure we have put on children has not actually led to a real improvement in standards. Sure, students are passing exams in increasing numbers but genuine studies of their attainment – such as the recent OECD report comparing educational systems in the developed world – reveal we are doing little better than we were 20 or 30 years ago, despite all the money pumped into the system.

If we are really going to improve things, we need to give our children an education which aims to stimulate their curiosity, to make them ask questions about the world around them, teach them stamina and staying power.

### Dealing with the tricky issues like sex, drugs and drink

In her misery memoir, *The Lost Child*, Julie Myerson describes every parent's nightmare: her once lovely son's descent into drug addiction. The book appears to show how her sweet-natured son, Jake, changed completely after he started smoking a particularly strong version of marijuana, nicknamed Skunk.

The drug seemed to drive him crazy. According to his mother, at one point he attempted to persuade his younger siblings to take the drug. On another occasion, he hit his mother, perforating her eardrum. Throughout most of his teens, he was uncooperative, aggressive, frequently violent and a nightmare to live with. Although a talented, articulate student at a high-achieving school, he dropped out completely, failing to take some of his GCSEs. When he was 17, after some particularly savage rows and fights, his parents chucked him out of the house – and changed the locks.

Myerson's message is clear: drugs ruin lives. In her book, she argues the case that the Skunk altered her son's brain so much that he turned from a civilised Dr Jekyll into a nightmarish Mr Hyde.

However, it is clear, from her own admission and subsequent interviews with her son, that this wasn't the whole story. Other factors came into play: the fractious relationship between his parents when Jake was 12, his feelings of alienation at school and his subsequent escape into drugs. Contrary to the stereotype, Jake wasn't offered drugs at his comprehensive: it was public-school students who he came to know outside school who encouraged him to smoke initially.

The Myerson story is instructive for a number of reasons. Firstly, it shows that drugs can affect any family – even the most educated and cultured. Secondly, it does reveal that while drugs may be dangerous, there are always other factors at play: regular drug-taking does not just happen for no reason. Children want to get out of their heads for a reason: unhappiness at home and school can play a big part. Thirdly and perhaps most crucially, it shows that talking about the issues early on is vital; parents can pay a heavy price for not paying enough attention to their children. Much of Jake's violent behaviour in the book could be interpreted as a bid for attention. His mother had been intending to go out on the night he perforated her eardrum. She was angry with him because he sat in the garden playing his electric guitar very loudly. An argument ensued and Jake said he would hit his mother if she took the guitar away from him. There was a tussle over the guitar and she was struck.

In the book, the Myersons are constantly threatening Jake. In my experience as a teacher, I've found threats don't work when you're dealing with very disaffected children: they just laugh at them. The only thing that works is listening and some genuine attention, talking through the issues, the problems, and being willing to tackle difficult issues. There are no easy solutions, but jaw-jaw is far better than war-war.

The attempts at zero tolerance that the Myersons tried after they'd allowed him to smoke in the house for years were futile. They didn't intervene early enough or address the root problems behind his drug-taking firmly enough. Their attempts at banning the drug later on were entirely counter-productive because he was too far down the road with his addiction.

There is no doubt that if your child wants to get drunk, get laid, and take drugs it's a hell of a lot easier than it used to be. This means that the 'prohibition' route that many parents take – banning them from attending certain social functions or seeing certain people – won't be that effective if they've got their own email account or mobile phone.

It is more important than ever that parents teach their children personal responsibility when it comes to drink, drugs and sex. That's very easy to say, but how is it done?

**Do:**
Set a good example yourself. If you drink/smoke heavily in front of your child, then he or she will probably do the same when given the chance.

Talk to your child about your fears. It is important to explain that you are frightened for them, and care for them, but try not to 'ban' them from doing things – all the evidence suggests that this approach backfires.

Keep them informed. Tell them the truth! Show them articles written by experts so that it's clear it's not just you who holds these views. Back up your points with hard evidence.

Set clear rules from the very start and be firm.

Use the web to keep up to date with the latest news on these subjects. The best place to start is the *Parentline Plus* which provides links to all the best websites dealing with these concerns. http://www.parentlineplus.org.uk/index.php?id=21 An organisation called DARE (Drugs Awareness Resistance Education) has been particularly effective in dealing with this problem. Their website is very good and provides much up-to-date information about various drugs. http://www.dare.uk.com/Pages/Static/AboutD.A.R.E.aspx

**Don't:**
Allow your child to take drugs in your house. It is against the law and if you sanction it you could get into trouble too. Don't fool yourself that it's better going on under your own roof. The slippery slope starts here. You send all the wrong signals if you accept illegal drug taking in your own home: you are telling your child that it's acceptable.

You may also be putting inadvertent pressure on them by

making your house the only 'drug' house of their peers; you'll find your house becomes a magnet, a badge of honour, a 'calling card' to be cool.

Overreact if they do take drugs or drink. Discuss the issues with them. Be firm that you don't want them taking the drugs but avoid drastic punishments. You need to encourage them to be sensible themselves, to regulate themselves, to look after themselves.

Don't cut off the lines of communication. The issues need to be talked through. As I said, jaw-jaw not war-war.

### Cyber-nightmares

Too many children's lives are being ruined by computers. The sheer amount of time that British children spend on the computer is staggering. On average children spend five hours and 18 minutes watching television, playing computer games or online each day. The total of 2,000 hours a year compares with 900 hours in class and 1,270 hours with their parents.[13]

When used properly, computers are a real boon, but parents have to talk through the risks involved with their children. This means asking your child about the games they play and warning them about possible dangers and pitfalls: the danger of chatting freely in chat-rooms and on social networking sites, the insidious way advertisers target children on the internet, and the materialistic world view it generates. With older children, it is probably necessary to talk about the violent images and pornography that they might see on the internet. Recent research suggests that boys in particular have their views of women shaped by what they see on the internet. Parents have a vital role to play in discussing these issues with their children. Most research shows that it is the children who have discussed sexual issues openly with their parents who are the least likely to have underage sex, pick up a sexually transmitted disease or get pregnant.

Teacher of the Year, Phil Beadle, is very suspicious of flashy technology. He told me: 'I see technology being treated as a universal panacea for every educational issue as idiotic. Shakespeare wrote all his plays with a feather quill from a ducks' arse. In fact, quite often the use of ICT in school is simply a means of a lazy teacher with a hangover getting through a lesson without effort or planning.

'If you want to do one thing for your child's education, take their computer games to the local dump. These decimate their attention spans, teach them the doctrine of violence as being acceptable, and make them try out kung fu moves in the most inappropriate settings. Learn to write with a pen or pencil first before you use a computer.'

**Do:**

Keep the computer in a communal area where everyone can see what is going on. Keep an eye on social networking sites and get regular updates from your child about what is going on.

Be positive about the genuinely good aspects of new technology: the easy access to information, the way the internet can bring boring subjects alive.

Be cautious and wary of advertisers on the internet.

Talk through some of the more troubling things that they might see on the internet: such as extreme violence or hardcore pornography.

---

13  *Consumer Kids: How big business is grooming our children for profit* by Ed Mayo and Agnes Nairn. Constable & Robinson (2009)

**Don't:**
Let them take expensive mobile phones or MP3 players to school.

Ban computers completely. Computers are here to stay. They can't be ignored.

# Bullying

*Only the best are bullied.* **Tim Field**[14]

## What good schools do about bullying

All good state schools are honest about the problem. Every good school now admits they have a problem with bullying because they realise that bullying is part of human nature. It happens everywhere and anywhere. But they also acknowledge that it has to be challenged and dealt with when it happens.

The main issue is this: you are always going to get bullying in any institution which is hierarchical and competitive. Even the best schools have their own hierarchies, their own unique forms of competition. This will inevitably engender feelings of insecurity, jealousy and aggression.

However, that said, many problems are not the school's fault at all and are brought in by children who are bullied by their parents at home.

As we will see there are many forms that bullying takes but

---

13  http://www.bullyonline.org/workbully/amibeing.htm

most bullies exhibit some very recognisable characteristics:

1 A very quick 'fuse' – bullies are easily annoyed
2 A thirst for control
3 A lack of empathy for their victims

Before I outline some ways to combat bullying, it is worth noting that there are a number of general principles that have to be employed in order to deal with bullying.

All good schools, whatever their way of dealing with the problem, will take these steps:

1 Listen carefully to anyone who complains or notices anything like bullying.
2 Investigate the problem in depth.
3 Discuss the problem with the bully and the bullies.
4 Suggest solutions.

Below are my unique interpretations and distillations of some of the ideas found in *Bullying – Brilliant ideas for keeping your child safe and happy* by Dr Sabina Dosani (Infinite Ideas, 2008). I have found this book very readable and realistic.

### How do good schools investigate bullying?

The best schools will be able to identify specific types of bullying and respond accordingly.

| Type of bully | Behaviours | Possible solutions |
|---|---|---|
| Manipulative bully | Very talkative, gossips maliciously, snubs and 'blanks' people, mocks and ridicules. | They want something: often attention, money, adulation, and acceptance. Addressing these concerns might help. |
| The 'Flashman' bully | Like Flashman in *Tom Brown's School Days*, this loud, yobbish bully uses his strength to push people around. | Lack of empathy is at the root of the problem here: getting the bully to consider other people's feelings can help if they are not a complete sociopath. |

# Bullying

| Type of bully | Behaviours | Possible solutions |
|---|---|---|
| The 'Special Needs' bully | Behind in their work, struggling to read and write properly, very angry about their lack of achievement. | Improving literacy and numeracy skills. Giving them work experience. See section on 'Young Apprenticeships' and vocational training. |
| The 'Victimised' bully | Believes they are always been picked up, will often talk about how everyone is bullying them while incessantly bullying others, they are slightly paranoid and over-sensitive, seeing slights and insults where they haven't happened. | Proper counselling can really help; a trained counsellor can unpick the reasons why the bully feels so 'victimised' and help him or her change their perceptions of the world |
| 'Gang' bullies | This is an organised group within a school who are finding a sense of family and kinship within a gang. Often they bond by carrying out criminal activities and may well be very secretive about their bullying. | Encouraging 'positive' families within a school such as sports' teams, artistic groups. |
| 'Yob' bullies | Unlike the 'gang' bullies, yobs are not organised but just brash and loud, revelling in theatrical displays of bullying. They are very keen to defend their 'manor' or territory. | Encouraging 'positive' forms of theatre: parades, celebrations, supervised parties. Encouraging 'positive' forms of 'appropriating' territory – encouraging murals rather than grafitti etc. |

## Spotting the signs of bullying

One of the worst things about bullying is that the victim often feels so ashamed that they don't want to tell anyone they are being bullied. You will need to spot the warning signs, which are numerous but can include:

- Any change in behaviour
- Shutting themselves away in their bedroom
- Being sullen and uncommunicative
- Acting aggressively
- Loss of appetite
- Binge eating
- Taking drugs
- Stealing
- Bruises
- Cuts
- Torn school clothes

## Technology

The internet has changed everything in terms of bullying. The explosion of social networking sites like Twitter, Facebook and MySpace have meant that children are in contact to a degree never seen before. Often children will have their whole year group on Twitter, MSN or Facebook; this makes it very easy for a bully to wage an intimidating campaign against someone they've got it in for. I've taught pupils who have been issued with death threats, been sent obscene and harrowing photos, threatened with beatings and called all the names under the sun. I've increasingly found that many pupils have become hardened to such experiences, not taking them seriously, seeing them as the banter that goes on; there is a sense that the internet is a forum where the usual rules do not apply, where things which would not be permitted face-to-face become acceptable in the virtual world. According to some statistics, as many as four out of ten pupils have been bullied online; this is a phenomenal number and it would be impossible for schools to deal with each case. As we will see later on, one of the best things parents can do is make sure that their children are sufficiently confident that they aren't devastated by stupid, idle threats and act calmly when they are confronted – because most likely they will encounter this. If it does, your child should save the offending email in a folder so that it can be shown to the technicians at school; often they can track down the source if it's come from a home computer.

I've had death threats sent to me over the internet and even 'hate' websites set up in my honour. My reaction has been to laugh. I've realised that if I tried to track down all the nasty stuff written about me on the internet I'd just waste hours of my time when I have far better things to do. Sometimes the best and simplest thing to do is switch the damn computer off. A further benefit in doing this is that it will stop your child becoming addicted to the computer – they can often shut themselves off from what is going on around them by just sitting on their computer in their bedroom; insisting that computers are kept in communal areas is another way around this. This also stops all sorts of other problems associated with the internet: illegal downloading, porngawping, and even frittering money away on your credit card!

**Solutions**

There are three key things to tell your child if they are being bullied:

1  It's not their fault. He or she has not brought it on themselves.
2  There are infinite solutions.
3  Don't fight back physically back *except in self-defence.*

I feel the last point is important because I have spoken to many parents who have told their children to fight back. All the research shows that this only increases the problem, with the victim frequently being excluded from school for fighting.

There are many solutions. The ones I have suggested here cover the following areas: body posture and self-defence, positive thinking, finding buddies, writing solutions, verbal solutions and technological solutions.

### Improving body posture and self-defence

Much research suggests that if children have good, confident body postures – walking confidently with their heads held high, striding purposefully, sitting up straight – this can counteract the effects of bullying.

Equally, learning self-defence can help. The best form of pre-emptive self-defence is the 'shield' or 'fence' where the flat of the hand is held out at arm's length whenever the bully tries to approach.

The ultimate form of self-defence is to run away – or, if the situation permits, to walk away. Ignoring a bully is powerful: 'blanking' them can work. Your child should not be ashamed of avoiding trouble.

### Positive mind-set

Encourage your child to take deep, long breaths when they feel stressed by situation, particularly when the bullying is going on. This sort of deep breathing is useful because it enables a bullied child to stop and think. If your child has time to think before acting then they will often make better decisions about how to deal with the bullying.

A positive mind-set can also help ease potential bullying situations. If your child learns to help other children without condition – it might be the bully or other pupils – by offering to help with work, or simply by being generous with their time or belongings, then the need for a bully-bullied scenario can be avoided.

Another way of being positive is to forgive the bully for being cruel. Forgiveness is a tremendously powerful way of overcoming negative feelings because it allows the bullied person to gain some control.

## Buddying solutions

Encouraging your child to find friends that might stay with them during the times when they are being bullied does work. You could help your child find a buddy by talking through with your child who their friends are. If he or she feels that they do not have any friends then talk about who might become their friends. Encourage your child to talk to them and ask for some company during break times, lessons, going to and from school. If your child really doesn't feel up to asking for a buddy then talk to your child's form tutor and get some help from the school.

Most schools now have mentoring schemes. Peer mentors can be very effective at stopping bullying, particularly if your child finds a responsible older child.

## Writing solutions

One of the most therapeutic ways of dealing with bullying is to encourage your child to write a diary. A place where they can write about all that has happened to them, and where their feeling and worries can be articulated.

Some schools have 'bully boxes' where pupils can post any thoughts and feelings, observations and experiences they have had of bullying anonymously. Ask your child's school to set one up if you think it might help.

Setting specific targets for each day can help too. For example, your child might write a few targets such as:

1  I will smile at my friends.
2  I will breathe in and out deeply when I meet the bully.
3  I will tell the teacher as soon as I can.

### Verbal solutions

Getting your child to think about what he or she might say to the bully can really help. Dosani notes that there are certain phrases that are worth saying when the bully issues his/her threats and taunts:

*Could you say that again?*

*I want you to stop saying that.*

*I want you to say that again so that the teacher hears you.*

*I want you to leave me alone.*

**Agreeing** can have the effect of diffusing the tension of a situation because it makes it clear that the bully's taunts are having no effect. Saying phrases, 'You're right, I'm an idiot. I'm a geek etc' can have the shock value to stop the bullying.

**Asking questions** can make a bully feel very uncomfortable. 'When you tell me that I'm a freak, could you tell me what you mean?'

**Laughing** at the situation is perhaps even more effective. I've noticed that time and time the jokers in a class consistently avoid being bullied.

### School solutions

Some schools tackle bullying with '**circle time**'. This is where pupils sit in a circle and discuss the bullying that's been going on without being rude to each other. Only one person is allowed to speak at a time and the whole thing is supervised by a teacher. It can be very effective if it is carried out in the right spirit; when pupils are reflective and rational, it can raise all sorts of issues which are tackled by being calm and imaginative. It can backfire badly though if it isn't run in the right way, especially when the teachers allow it to become unruly. Then it can become a nightmare for the victim because the 'circle time' itself becomes a form of bullying as past incidents are raked over.

Perhaps the opposite of the 'No Blame' approach is a '**Bully Court**' where pupils and teachers devise a way of putting the bullies on trial; this concept is predicated on the notion that the bully will ultimately be judged and given a definite punishment. Just as important as holding the 'trial' of a bully is involving pupils in setting up a fair form of justice so that everyone's rights are respected: indeed these discussions could resolve much because at the heart of the problem of most bullying is how justice is achieved. Sometimes the most successful 'Bully Courts' are actually ones that never happen because pupils have resolved their issues in discussing ways in which the trial could run and then realised that they have, in fact, already achieved their purpose: made the bully realise the error of his/her ways and achieved some sense of justice for the victim.

I've found that things like 'circle time' and the 'Bully Court' can be effective, but more often than not it is only when adults become actively involved that things are really sorted out. Trained counsellors can be very effective in helping victims and bullies deal with the central problems. Equally, GPs are now trained to deal with bullying issues.

Concerned teachers can set up certain '**trust games**' which often help children build up empathy for other children. Asking pairs and groups to do jigsaws silently can encourage co-operation and important eye-contact that can eradicate bullying.

Equally, drama activities such as improvisations based around bullying situations can help make children think about the emotional consequences of bullying.

State schools themselves all have clear 'chains of command' when dealing with disciplinary issues. Learning to **go up the chain** properly can be effective instead of immediately calling the headteacher about bullying. Usually, you should start off by contacting the form tutor: this is the teacher who registers your child and looks after their well-being in school. If the form tutor is good and willing to take the time to investigate the problem then you may find the problem solved then and there. If not, see your child's head of year. If there's still no joy, contact the deputy headteacher and, finally, the headteacher. After that, if the school has been really ineffective make a complaint to the governing body of the school.

One last resort is to call the **police,** particularly if your child is receiving death threats or is being badly beaten up. The police take bad cases of bullying seriously and will prosecute the offenders if necessary.

You could also think about changing schools if your child is suffering at the hands of a bully, and all other tactics have failed.

# Special Needs

*Constantly late for school, losing his books and
papers and various other things into which I need not enter.
He is so regular in his irregularity that I really don't know
what to do.* **Winston Churchill's school report**

### What are 'special educational needs'?

Definition: The term Special Educational Needs, or SEN, denotes children of school age in the UK who have learning difficulties or disabilities that make it harder for them to learn than children who are not designated as SEN.

It's an absurd term because, as any parent knows, all children have 'special needs', that is, 'needs' which are 'special' or unique to them. Not so long ago, right-thinking professionals called children 'retarded', 'thick', 'stupid', 'dim' or 'slow', but now they all say that children have 'Special Educational Needs'.

As a result, a lot of parents feel insulted when their child is labelled as having 'special needs'. They shouldn't, though. In fact, quite the opposite! There is a strong case to be made that all parents who don't have their child labelled as SEN should be knocking on any teacher's door they can find and clamouring for them to pin this wonderful sobriquet on their charge's foreheads. Children with SEN may be finding it difficult to learn to read, to write, to do their arithmetic; they may be struggling to explain themselves clearly or discuss issues with their peers. The bottom line is: SEN means more attention, more money, and much more preferential treatment. If your child has any kind of learning difficulty you should flag it up with the school and KEEP ALL THE PAPERWORK!

At the moment, although the issue has been with us since schools started, the 'science' of Special Needs is only just being addressed: new qualifications are being set up so that teachers can be properly trained in the relevant areas and new research is beginning to unmask what learning difficulties exist and how to tackle them. Meanwhile, many teachers and schools are still groping their way forward, doing things by trial and error. My experience is that there are huge gaps in our knowledge and it is only if parents are on the ball and a bit pushy that their children will get the attention they deserve.

## How will swatting up on the SEN jargon help my child?

It is key to remember that the whole realm of SEN is a very nebulous and ill-defined one. Most SEN Coordinators (SENCOs: in charge of ensuring that every pupil who has special needs in the school gets the right attention) have not taken a degree in a relevant subject such as Child Psychology but have come into the job because they are 'good with difficult kids'.

No one quite knows exactly what a 'learning difficulty' is. You will know better than 99% of teachers whether your child has one. The bottom line with SEN is this:

1 If you suspect anything, discuss it with the SENCO.

**2** In many cases, parent's concerns are brushed aside because dealing with SEN involves quite a bit of paperwork and effort on the SENCO's behalf. So be pushy. Insist that your child is properly assessed.

**3** If your child is assessed by the school or the Local Authority and nothing is done, take it a step further by talking to your local Parent Partnership.

## CASE STUDY  The story of Josh

Recently, talking late in the evening to parents of 16-year-old GCSE students, I was struck by the lack of knowledge there was on SEN issues. In particular, one parent, Mrs Smith, had developed a stress-related rash because her 16-year-old son, Josh, was doing so badly in school. In his Key Stage 3 English test, taken a couple of years previously, he had only managed a Level 3, and, just a couple of months ago in his mock English GCSE, he attained an 'F' grade. I explained that I thought he had a 'special educational need'; he was displaying the symptoms of 'dysgraphia': the inability to express himself while writing by hand (see the check list below). After his mother kicked up a real fuss, he was assessed by the borough's SENCO and an educational psychologist. The ed psych felt Josh didn't have 'dysgraphia' because he applied a very narrow definition of the term. He defined 'dysgraphia' as when a child's writing is totally illegible – other educational psychologists apply the term more broadly. But more importantly, my use of the term in Josh's case *did* make the powers-that-be sit up, and it got Josh an assessment. He was judged to be a 'slow' handwriter, meaning in this context that he had a learning difficulty: his handwriting meant that he had difficulty accessing the mainstream curriculum.

As a result, after much lobbying by his mother and the SEN department, funds were found to give him a laptop to use in lessons and exams. Subsequently, his results improved dramatically. However, it took a lot of hard work to get him the laptop. His mother couldn't afford one and initially the SEN department were reluctant to pay for a new one. Josh was just one of many who needed extra resources. Nevertheless when I was able to prove that it would make the difference between Josh attaining F grades in his GCSEs and C grades, the department sat up and listened. It wasn't easy, but we got there in the end.

What seems incredible to me is that Josh's 'learning difficulties' were not picked up much sooner. By the time he was eight, it should have been clear to his teachers that he had some difficulties with his handwriting which were severely hampering his progress. However, parents like Josh's mum – from more deprived backgrounds – don't always know how to support their children fully. She hadn't been pushy at his primary school and had not demanded that Josh be given a clear plan of action for improvement. Instead, he had drifted from year to year feeling more and more demoralised and mucking around in class as a result.

Josh's case is very important because it illustrates two vital factors in the success of a child at school: the importance of early assessment and parental input. Josh is one of the lucky ones; he is naturally bright and so with a laptop he has been able to pass most exams. However, many children who come from deprived backgrounds enter primary school far more inarticulate than Josh. Studies have shown that children whose parents are living on benefits are not exposed to the language that the children of affluent parents are. One fascinating piece of research conducted in the US a few years ago showed that on average, when in the company of their parent, a 'middle class' child listens and responds to a thousand more words per hour than a child living with a single parent on welfare; by the age of three it was estimated that a middle-class child would have been exposed to 35 million words, while a child on welfare is exposed to just 10 million.

Linguistic impoverishment plays a huge factor in a child's attainment at school. And yet many schools are simply not equipped to cope with children who cannot communicate coherently; the Key Stage tests at seven do not adequately diagnose what is wrong with them and the curriculum is not designed to give these children the intensive language training they need. However, studies in the US and the UK show when children are given intensive 'communication' catch-up programmes very early on in their school career – in reception and Year 1 – the impact has been huge. They have gone on to achieve well as teenagers.

Josh's problem was not severe because he was articulate; when given the tools to express himself in writing, he was able to shine. However, I have taught many pupils who have had multiple special needs: just looking at the list below will show you how many there are. In my experience, many children are not being diagnosed as SEN or, if they are, the programme of action they are given does not help them. What most of them need is an intensive communication training in their primary schools. Without this, they enter secondary school unable to cope with the curriculum; unable to discuss things in a sustained fashion or to understand properly what is going on. With little or no support at home and teachers' hands tied by a restrictive National Curriculum which doesn't allow enough time to give extra 'communication' lessons, they then fail to gain the five A*-C grades at GCSE that the government expects all pupils to achieve.

The lesson is this: if their school or their parents had been tuned into SEN properly, they would not have failed. Parents must not be ashamed of having their child labelled SEN; it is not a badge of shame, it is a useful label that enables your school to ask for extra resources to help them learn in a more productive way.

**Some common SEN terms to learn and love – why jargon opens doors (and purses)**

The moment a SEN teacher has a technical term with which to describe a learning difficulty, they feel much, much happier. Words like 'dyslexia', 'dyspraxia' and 'dysgraphia' mean a SENCO can apply for a specialist to look at a pupil, and can use it in a report or Individual Education Plan to justify giving extra help and money to a pupil. The truth is, however, that these technical terms are very vague; even if a specialist disagrees with you and says your child doesn't have the condition, you can *still* argue the toss for him or her to be put on School Action or School Action Plus.

**Attention Deficit Hyperactivity Disorder**

This is when your child finds it difficult to concentrate upon anything for more than a few seconds. They may be very restless, extremely easily distracted, unable to focus upon any task, even watching the TV may be difficult for them. Children with the condition may be clumsy, and constantly looking for attention.

For more information, look at Mind's booklet on the issue: http://www.mind.org.uk/Information/Booklets/Understanding/Understanding+ADHD.htm

**Auditory processing disorder**

This is when a child may have difficulty listening and taking in more complicated instructions. It may be that they learn better when instructions are written down or put in diagram form for them.

**Autism spectrum disorder**

This is a neurological disorder that causes a range of psychological conditions, but the key behavioural anomaly to look for is how your child interacts with other people: if they display 'abnormal' behaviour when interacting, and communicate in a different fashion to others. Children with the disorder often have very restricted interests and exhibit highly repetitive behaviour.

For more information, look at the National Autistic Society's website: http://www.nas.org.uk/

### Obsessive-compulsive disorder

This is when children have no control over their thoughts and feel compelled to think and act in extremely rigid, repetitive patterns such as insisting upon washing their hands repeatedly, obsessively putting objects in straight lines, repeating certain words or phrases.

For more information see:
http://www.mind.org.uk/Information/Booklets/Understanding/Understanding+obsessive-compulsive+disorder.htm


### Learning difficulties related to reading

**Dyslexia.** This is the most common label applied to children with learning difficulties. The phrase itself has many meanings and definitions depending upon who you talk to. Some specialists interpret it very precisely as a neurological disorder resulting in great difficulty forming correct spellings and decoding writing; these specialists will look for specific 'dysfunctions' in the process of reading and spelling in order to diagnose whether someone suffers from it. Other people see it as a general blanket term for any kind of reading and spelling difficulty. The key thing for parents to remember is that ANY KIND of reading difficulty is a learning difficulty. It doesn't matter whether your child's condition is diagnosed as dyslexia or given the phrase 'reading disability', it is still a learning difficulty – and they are entitled to extra support as a result. The most common kind of reading difficulty is a pupil's inability to break up words into 'phonemes' – or units of sounds – when reading. This is often because they haven't been very well taught. A great deal of research evidence suggests that all children should be taught 'synthetic phonics'; i.e they need to be taught how various letters and letter combinations create sounds before they are given texts to read properly. A good school will give children in their early years plenty of flash-cards where they learn all these sounds and relate them to the relevant letters. Your child should have been taught about:

**Blends.** In other words, they should know how to draw individual sounds together to pronounce a word, e.g. t-r-ee, blended together, reads tree

**Phonemes.** They should know these are the smallest single identifiable sounds, e.g. the letters 'sh' represent just one sound, but 'sp' represents two (/s/ and /p/)

**Graphemes.** They should know that written symbols are the equivalent of sounds (a grapheme is a written symbol that is used to represent speech). They should be aware that groups of letters can represent one sound. For example, 'ough' is the equivalent of 'o' in words like 'though'.

**Digraphs.** They should know that two letters can make one sound, e.g. *sh, ch, th, ph*. Vowel digraphs comprise two vowels which, together, make one sound, e.g. *ai, oo, ou*

If they have significant difficulty in decoding these letter patterns, then they will probably have a reading disability, and you should urgently be asking for an SEN assessment. Remember, these sorts of reading disabilities can be left undiagnosed throughout a pupil's school career; it is never too late to ask for advice. I have taught GCSE students who still struggled with their digraphs and their graphemes – once they were taught them properly, they were fine, but they had drifted through years of school without getting any support, struggling at their reading and failing in most of their subjects as a results.

For more information on the government's thinking about reading, check out the Rose review which showed definitively that all pupils need to be taught synthetic phonics at an early age:
http://www.standards.dcsf.gov.uk/phonics/rosereview/

### Learning difficulties related to writing

**Dysgraphia.** Some specialists use 'dysgraphia' as an overarching term to describe any problems with handwriting, spelling, organisation of ideas, and composition. Others, such as the International Dyslexia Association, use the word exclusively to describe difficulties with handwriting. I think it is useful to use it in its most general usage because it sounds impressive. I know from experience that SENCOs and LA advisors sit up and listen when the term is used; it is a technical term to be reckoned with, and it gives specialists an anchor from which they can steady their ship.

**Dyslexia.** This term is used not only when a pupil has difficulty reading (see above) but also when he or she has real problems with spelling. Writing disabilities are very common but often overlooked. The skills required to write are even more advanced than those for reading. A pupil who has writing disabilities may have:

**Weak motor skills.** Their hand-eye co-ordination may mean they struggle to write more than a few words or sentences. I have taught a number of pupils who found the process of handwriting very difficult but thrived when they had a laptop or a scribe to assist them.

**A poor appreciation of context, audience and purpose.** Here pupils who are on the autism spectrum really struggle, not understanding why they are writing or whom they are writing for.

**Poor organisational skills.** Many writers have lots of thoughts but struggle to put them in a coherent fashion on the page. They may have learning difficulties relating to their 'cognitive organisational skills' which they could need extra help with. In particular, having extra help with planning work really can improve their work.


## Learning difficulties related to maths

**Dyscalculia.** This is another over-arching phrase that sounds very impressive. It basically describes any kind of problem that your child might have with the basic mathematical concepts such as: quantity, place value, and time; memorising mathematical facts such as times tables, the organisation of numbers, and understanding how problems are arranged and sequenced on the page.

**Non-verbal learning disabilities.** This is another huge area covering such wide-ranging problems as: poor visual-spatial skills, emotional behavioural problems, problems with maths and lack of organisational skills. You will need to contact your school's SENCO if your child has any of these problems. Possibly the most problematic are 'emotional behavioural' difficulties which are stopping your child learning; it may be that they react angrily to the prospect of learning anything, or they are getting into fights with their peers, or they are finding it very difficult to make friends.

Children on the **autistic spectrum** often exhibit these sorts of problems. However, these children may also excel in other areas, such as learning by rote memory.

**Dyspraxia.** This is when a child has severe difficulty in drawing, writing, doing up buttons, and other tasks requiring fine motor skills, or in sequencing the necessary movements. Moreover, they may have difficulty doing simple movements such as waving goodbye or more involved tasks such as brushing their teeth or getting dressed. Children with this condition may frequently be labelled as 'clumsy' because they find it difficult to work out spatial relationships.

For more information read: *Dyspraxia – Developmental Co-ordination Disorder*, A Parents' Guide From Pre-school to Adulthood by Dr Amanda Kirby (Souvenir Press, 2006).

**CASE STUDY    What could I have done to get more support for my son's dyspraxia?**
Although clearly a very bright boy, Jason, the son of a merchant banker and a solicitor, had struggled throughout his time at primary school. He had learnt to read very quickly, but by Year 4, when he was eight, he was still struggling to write more than a few sentences: his handwriting was frequently unreadable. During the mornings, he would take a very long time to get dressed and he found it impossible to keep his room remotely tidy: flinging his toys, clothes and books randomly in a pile. His teacher suggested a referral to the SENCO but his parents, worried that he would be labelled 'thick', resisted and instead hired a private tutor to help him with his writing. His progress with his writing remained painfully slow.

If things were bad at primary school, at secondary school things got a lot worse. Still finding it difficult to get dressed quickly and not being able to put his school bag together properly, Jason suffered a great deal: he often was late and failed to bring the right books to class, achieving low marks in his work despite having a very high level of understanding. A more forceful teacher at the secondary school insisted he was assessed for Special Needs. The SENCO immediately put him on School Action, diagnosing him as having mild to moderate dyspraxia. The immediate result of this was that he was given a laptop in class and provided with some typing lessons to help him improve his speed. In the next few months, his work improved greatly: his typed responses were much more detailed than anything he had done before. Problems with his organisation remained, however, and it was decided to move him to School Action Plus, with a Local Authority assessment.

An educational psychologist judged that he needed some very clear guidance and training with his organisation. Even with things like getting dressed, he needed to have a clear set of instructions written down for him. He needed to pack his school things into his bag the night before. More significantly, he was given some classes to assist him with his motor skills: how to do his shoelaces, how to hold a pen, how to cut and chop vegetables, how to cook. These helped. But it was clear that years of struggling and being misunderstood had led him to being quite an angry and frustrated child: his impatience with himself continued to cause huge temper tantrums. A fight in school led him to being excluded. He was assessed by the educational psycho-logist again and it was decided that he should have some 'anger-management' classes. His teachers were also trained about how to respond to him appropriately: they shouldn't try and hurry him, but give him clear instructions about what he should do next.

In the end, the SEN support worked and Jason attained eight good GCSEs, four A Levels and went onto study Politics at university. Having taught him in Year 7 and then again a year or two later, I saw just how effective the intervention was: from being an angry, frustrated 11-year-old, he became a confident, high-achieving student. All thanks to a correct diagnosis of 'dyspraxia'.

## Learning difficulties related to speaking and listening

Signs that your child might have this learning difficulty are:

Poor memory
Difficulty in making friends and interacting with people
Organising their time – poor punctuality, being slow at apparently simple things like getting dressed, or packing their school bag.

Basically, the rule is: if you notice ANYTHING, bring it up with the SENCO or relevant teacher. If in doubt, get it checked out! The earlier this disability is caught the better, and there are specialists who can really turn this problem around. Recent research conducted by the NHS has shown that speech therapy for children as young as five can significantly improve speaking and listening skills. You will need to be pushy with your child's school to make sure your child gets assessed properly and is then given regular speech therapy. It will dramatically improve their prospects, and put them on track to thrive.

## What happens when my child is diagnosed as having SEN?

If you and the school feel that your child has 'special needs' then they will be given an 'Individual Education Plan', this is quite a detailed document – different from the Individual Action Plan which all pupils are entitled to and can be quite brief – in which the school, parent and pupil outline the things that will be done to help them improve. In the jargon, this stage is known as 'School Action'. The IEP should suggest specific ways of teaching which will help them: for example, they may need to use colours, drawings, mnemonics etc to help them remember certain spellings or vocabulary. It should also state what extra help they will get in class; the idea at this point will be to keep them in the class as much as possible. Deadlines will also be provided, to ensure that the school checks that the IEP is working.

If the IEP doesn't work, your child is entitled to move onto 'School Action Plus'. This is when the school will talk to an outside agency to see how they might help. Working with this agency, the school will draw up a new IEP to include the help from outside the school.

Ultimately, if the 'School Action Plus' fails, you are entitled to apply to your Local Authority to have your child assessed formally for a 'statement of Special Needs'; your LA has to respond to you within six weeks. If your LA agrees to help, it will give your child a 'statutory assessment'. This is a very detailed investigation into your child – and unsurprisingly an excessively bureaucratic and time-consuming procedure. Everyone and their dog are consulted: you, a doctor, an educational psychologist, social services if they know of your child, and any other relevant person in your LA. After all this consultation, a 'statement of special needs' is produced, a big document which outlines a clear set of targets for the various agencies involved, you and your child to attend to. Your child should be given extra resources and teaching, all of which is laid out clearly in the statement.

If your LA decides not to assess your child for a statement, then you should go back to the school in the first instance and ask for their advice. You also have a right to appeal to the Special Educational Needs and Disability Tribunal, an independent organisation. It is important that you begin any appeal to the Tribunal within the time limit given, as this body is likely to refuse to hear your appeal if you are late (see http://www.sendist.gov.uk/ for more details).

The government has produced a guide to SEN for parents, which is quite useful and shows that you have many more rights than you might expect: http://www.teachernet.gov.uk/doc/3755/parents-carers_PRESS%20READY.pdf

**Do:**

Be open-minded about special needs.

Talk through any concerns you have with your child's teachers.

Ask for extra help and resources.
Get to know the jargon a bit.

Be pro-active straightaway. If your child is struggling, contact your child's teachers a.s.a.p.

**Don't:**

Be ashamed of the special needs label. There was a time when it carried a stigma, but it doesn't now.

Suffer in silence. Talk the problems through.

### Did school make Jade thick?

Jade Goody's appearances on *Big Brother* and the tragic drama of her death from cancer, played out in the full glare of the media, have made her perhaps the most famous 'intellectually challenged' person in Britain. On *Big Brother*, first in 2002 and then in 2007, she made some comments which have caused her name to be synonymous with stupidity. Her ill-educated sayings include:

- Do they speak Portuguese in Portugal?
- I thought Portugal was in Spain.
- Rio de Janeiro, ain't that a person?
- Where is East Angular, is it abroad?
- Saddam Hussein – that's a boxer.
- Sherlock Holmes invented toilets.
- Mother Theresa is from Germany.

While her lack of geographical and general knowledge definitely indicate that she received a very rudimentary academic education, her racist remarks about her contestant Shilpa Shetty during the 2007 *Celebrity Big Brother* revealed her moral education to be even worse. She sparked an international incident, causing riots in India when she called Shetty 'Shilpa Poppadom' and 'Shilpa Fuckawala'.

Was it Jade's schooling that was at fault here? Clearly, Jade herself thought so and in a bid to stop her sons making the same mistake she decided to send them to private schools.

The daughter of a drug-addict who was jailed for armed robbery and a mother who was frequently in trouble with the police for petty misdemeanours, Jade grew up in Bermondsey, south London, and attended St James's Primary School. There, according to her autobiography, she gained a plump boyfriend with freckles and played kiss-chase and 'Cat's Got the Measles'. Her happiest time at school seems to have been the school trips she went on – in particular, a trip to Nethercot Farm, where the children learned to muck out all the animals, collect eggs from a chicken hut and feed the sheep.

The behaviour of Jade's mother resulted in Jade having to move schools quite a bit. At one school, Jade was expelled after her mother punched a teacher. This happened because Jade was apparently told that she was not allowed to join a lesson because she was a 'brown girl'. Infuriated by this racist insult, her mother had stomped into school and assaulted the teacher.

Jade was kicked out of another school because her mother hit another pupil's mother. She was six years old when a girl had touched her in the school toilets and made supposedly suggestive comments about how they should play doctors and nurses. When her mother learned of this, she embroiled herself in a huge contretemps with the other girl's mother – and Jade being asked to leave the school.

In another school, a supply teacher allegedly patted Jade on the bottom; Jade spent the rest of the lesson pinging pieces of paper at him. As a punishment, she was sent by the irate teacher to the headmistress. Jade promptly informed her that the teacher was a pervert. This time she wasn't punished – it was the teacher who was sacked.

She attended a secondary school called Bacon's College where she was quite good at maths but hated English, never learning how to punctuate or spell. Her homework was handed back covered in red ink. Comments such as 'See me', 'Stay behind', or 'Need to discuss' were often written at the bottom of her work, but they seemed to have little effect in motivating Jade to work harder. While her writing was poor, she seems to have enjoyed reading. Not surprisingly, geography appears to have been her worst subject. Her school reports said that she talked too much, rarely concentrated and that she was 'dominating' – teacher-talk for being a bully. Most of her school life seems to have been consumed by boys, clothes and socialising. The only positive educational experiences she had were after school when she attended dance classes, which she enjoyed greatly, winning a number of trophies.

Not learning much in lessons and failing to attend the revision classes laid on by the school, Jade got very poor GCSE results; mostly E and U grades. She slept through one of her maths exams. Needless to say, after this she left school, taking a succession of menial jobs before she auditioned successfully for *Big Brother*.

It is clear that a toxic brew of a disturbed home life, Jade's own lack of interest in studying and the rigidity of the British education system led to her failing miserably at school. Her tale is instructive in many ways. For all we may laugh at her lack of general knowledge, Jade was clearly a bright woman who could, if given the right education, have succeeded at school. Her lack of success highlights why many children fail at school. Our Victorian curriculum failed to teach her the basics of reading, writing and arithmetic. If she'd been able to pursue further her interest in dance and drama, on the other hand, and had learnt to read and write within the context of these subjects, taking good vocational qualifications in them, then she might have been motivated to learn. In other words, with a curriculum which interested her, which was tailored more to her interests and passions, she would have succeeded.

I know this is the case because I teach a few 'Jades' at the moment; girls who are obsessed by movies, make-up, clothes, boys and musicals. Generally, they are very reluctant to knuckle down to reading antiquated literature, but really come alive in the media classes I teach. They've loved writing scripts, devising storyboards and shooting movies based on their own interests – and they've learnt more English in the process than they ever did when I attempted to teach them Thomas Hardy's *Far From The Madding Crowd.*

If Jade's learning had been 'practical' and responsive, then she would have been properly educated. To that extent, school *did* make Jade thick.

If you are interested in learning more about practical learning of the sort that might have motivated Jade, log onto: http://www.edge.co.uk/docs/home/

Edge is an organisation devoted to promoting practical learning in schools and colleges.

## Gifted and Talented

For many concerned middle-class parents, 'Gifted and Talented' (G&T) is a very important issue. Basically, if a school judges your child to be 'G&T' then there is a chance for him or her to attend extra classes free of charge. Of particular value are any G&T classes in maths and science – two subjects which state schools are notoriously poor at teaching in mainstream classes.

You see, 'Gifted and talented' describes children with an

ability to develop to a level significantly ahead of their year group but this doesn't have to be in all subject areas. For example, it may be that your child is particularly talented at art or drama, but not particularly good at maths or science.

## How do I know if my child is G&T?

As with SEN, it is worth your while being very pushy! If your child hasn't been identified by the School Census as being G&T, ask his or her teachers to assess him, pointing out the areas that he is good at. In my experience, many teachers are rather flummoxed by the whole G&T area and will often simply bung down the names of those pupils who have come top of the relevant tests. This can be a mistake because some G&T pupils don't do very well at tests but are definitely G&T: I can think of one boy I taught, nicknamed 'Moose', a huge hulking crate of a boy who always did badly in tests because his writing was terrible, but who was extremely articulate and incisive: he was G&T but never was put down for any courses because of his poor test scores and bad behaviour. I regret now not putting him on the register myself because he dropped out of school and, as far as I know, hasn't done much since.

So the rule is: if in doubt, be pushy; demand that your child is assessed, think of any areas that might be relevant. Remember the whole thing is extremely vague so you should consider your child's talents in things like:

- Leadership skills
- Communication skills
- Creative thinking
- Critical thinking
- All the academic subjects
- Sport
- Music
- Drama

You should contact your child's teacher, or the headteacher if you feel he or she is G&T. Every school should have a an individual dedicated to keep abreast of this area, called a 'Leading Teacher for G&T', although some smaller schools may share their Leading Teacher. This person should be organising extra activities and advertising all the relevant courses that are on offer.

**What happens after my child is identified as G&T?**
Your child should get extra classes and support! This should happen within school – during classes teachers should make sure that your child is doing work that really stretches him or her – and outside the normal curriculum time. There is also the Young Gifted and Talented programme (YG&T), which was set up in 2007 to provide support and opportunities for gifted and talented children aged four to 19, including those who were members of the former National Academy for Gifted and Talented Youth (NAGTY). The YG&T Learner Academy should run loads of courses which are designed to stretch and challenge kids. These courses can be held 'online' as well as at eduational venues.

**Do:**
Remember that if your child is not being stretched at school, you should contact his tutor/head of year/ headteacher immediately and ask for him/her to have a clear plan of action for improvement (Individual Action Plan).

Be aware that if your child goes to a school with high levels of 'low' achievement, pressing for him to be put on the G&T register is a good way of helping him get the extra support he will need to attain at the top levels. Interestingly, many inner city schools are very appreciative of  G&T students and there are far better programmes at these schools than in the more suburban schools.

Check out the relevant websites: The National Association for Gifted Children's website, http://www.nagcbritain.org.uk advertises all the national courses that are on offer and has plenty of advice for parents. The website for the Young Gifted & Talented (YG&T) programme (http://ygt.dcsf.gov.uk) which aims to give all gifted and talented learners in England the opportunity to reach their full potential is also useful.

Encourage your child to take up a musical instrument: music has been proven to develop intelligence and constantly challenges children.

**Don't:**
Sit around and moan. Work with the school to make sure your child is challenged and stretched.

## Setting and streaming

Keeping an eye on what set or band your child is in is very important in secondary school. It could affect the exams that he or she is entered for. In particular, it may affect whether your child is entered for a higher or lower tier in their GCSE exams. If your child is entered for a lower tier GCSE, this usually means that he cannot attain above a grade C in his GCSE.

If you are worried about the set your child is in, you should follow these steps.

**Do:**
Ask to see all the relevant test data that the school has on your child. In particular, ask to see the results of any IQ (Intelligence Quotient) tests which your child has. Many schools, distrustful of the Key Stage test results, pay for companies to do multiple-choice IQ-style tests (the names vary according to the company carrying out the testing) to see what a pupil's IQ looks like. It may be that your child

has scored poorly on these tests and has been put in a lower set or stream as a result of this. In which case, question the result! IQ tests are still a very controversial area: they usually fail to take into account a child's creativity and social skills and instead focus upon a narrow range of skills such as their mathematical ability, their verbal knowledge, their spatial knowledge and their reasoning skills. The best schools will always look at a number of test scores and take into account the teacher assessment of a child. The most accurate assessment is usually the teacher's although there is a caveat. If there has been pressure on a teacher to inflate their scores – which in these days of performance-related pay is always a problem – then the teacher's assessment must also be regarded warily.

Examine the social, gender and ethnic mix of a particular group or set. Equal opportunities legislation these days means that all classes should reflect the ethnic, social and gender mix of the school as a whole. I have had to teach some disastrous bottom sets made up solely of white working class and Afro-Caribbean boys, some of whom were pretty clever but who had been placed in the bottom set because of their atrocious behaviour. You are within your rights to ask that your child is moved to a class which properly reflects the social mix of the school.

**Don't:**
Involve your child in all your inquiries by denigrating the set they are in. It may be that they will have to stay there. If you have done nothing but attack the group to your child, or allowed your child to indulge in moaning endlessly about it, then you will not have done them any favours if they are forced to stay there.

# Assessment

*I made my own assessment of my life, and I began to live it.*
*That was freedom.* **Fernando Flores**

**Introduction – A short history of British examinations**
In 1918 the Higher School Certificate was introduced for school leavers; it was usually taken at the age of 18.

The 11-plus was created as part of the Butler Education Act 1944 and still exists as a test for entrance to grammar schools; it tests verbal and non-verbal reasoning, mathematics and writing.

O-levels (Ordinary levels) were introduced in the 1950s as subject-based qualifications under a General Certificate of Education, to test 16-year-olds on academic knowledge. Between 1965 and 1987, there was also a Certificate of Secondary Education (CSE) designed to assess those pupils in England, Wales and Northern Ireland who did not take GCE O-levels.

In 1986 both O-levels and CSEs were replaced by GCSEs (the General Certificate of Secondary Education).

A-levels were introduced in 1951, replacing the Higher

School Certificate, to test students in academic subjects at the end of the sixth form.

In 2000, A-levels were reformed and AS-levels were created, to test students at the end of their first year in the sixth form. At the same time, A-levels became 'modular': each A-level consisting of six modules, tested either by coursework or by examination, enabling pupils to retake modules if necessary. A-levels were reformed again this year, the number of modules being cut from six to four.

At primary school level, Key Stage tests and school league tables based on their results were introduced in the 1990s. KS1 tests for seven-year-olds are in reading, writing and maths, and also offer teacher assessments in science. KS2 tests (for 11-year-olds) cover English, maths and science, as did the old KS3 tests for 14-year-olds – in October, the government announced the end of testing for 14-year-olds, to be replaced by teacher assessments.

## My adventures in the testing trade

The decision by the Children's Secretary, Ed Balls, to kill off the tests for 14-year-olds was arguably one of the most momentous taken by a politician during Gordon Brown's tenure as prime minister.

Dramatic as it may sound, I believe the scrapping of these wretched exams will have far greater long-term repercussions than the bailing out of the banks.

As a middle-aged teacher who has taught for nearly two decades in state schools, I have had my life transformed. For 16 years, I have been penned up in sweaty classrooms drilling bored teenagers through the pointless complexities of the English SATs papers.

I have watched some pupils bow their heads and scribble dutifully over them, while others turn them into paper aeroplanes. I have gone home every day worrying about how I might improve my results in that year's test. In my most depressed moments, *my* life has felt like one long, sad SATs test.

When the Education Act of 1988 introduced the concept of Standard Attainment Tests – SATs, also known as Key Stage tests – I, as a young teacher, cheered. In common with most of my colleagues, I supported the notion of testing our children in a regular and organised way.

In theory, SATs appeared eminently sensible: Key Stage 1 and 2 tests would assess seven- and 11-year-olds mainly in reading, writing and arithmetic, while Key Stage 3 tests would have equal components of testing in English, maths and science. Children would be assigned levels from 1-7, which were standardised across the whole age range, and therefore parents, pupils and teachers could see clearly whether students were progressing at the expected rate; if a pupil did not move up at least one or two levels between each stage then alarm bells would ring.

In practice, however, these tests have proved to be nightmarish failures. The SATs have not only led to a marked decline in standards, they have broken children's zeal for learning. They have alienated pupils, teachers and parents alike without making schools properly accountable.

The root of the problem is this: the SATs have made children better at passing abstruse exams but in so doing have wiped out all enthusiasm for learning, leaving them lacking in initiative, unable to construct sustained arguments and powerless to think imaginatively.

At a stage in their education when pupils could be reading great literature in English, exploring the wonder of numbers in maths, understanding the forces of the universe in science, they have instead been plodding through tedious practice papers and learning the wording of the relevant mark schemes.

They have not been educated; they have been trained simply to jump through the hoops of the exams.

The KS1 and 2 tests were supposed to give accurate information about pupils' proficiency in the three Rs. However, as an English teacher who was expected to use the KS1 and 2 English scores to inform his teaching, I soon noticed that the levels the pupils were arriving with from their primary schools were inaccurate. More worryingly, the method of 'teaching to the test' seemed to have sapped the confidence and passion of children as young as 11.

I can vividly remember, five years ago, my new Year 7 pupils groaning when they saw that they would be reading a novel with me at the beginning of the year.

'Do we have to read books?' a blond-haired boy named Liam asked me during the first week of term.

I had never encountered such resistance to learning before. But then I reflected that he was one of the first pupils who had known nothing but SATs teaching since he was six years old. T he effect was shocking: 11-year-old children, who had in previous years been eager to learn, were now jaded and moaning about work, fighting and giggling in class, writing only short answers and struggling to read anything that wasn't on a test paper. It was only when I set them a mock test that they shut up and got on with some work: it was the only form of education they understood.

Having been drilled to answer questions on little bites of text, too many children were unable to read longer books independently. Moreover, they seemed utterly disillusioned by the prospect of studying English. Liam sneered at everything put before him until he brought in his own crime novel from home.

In desperation, I allowed him to read it even though it wasn't on the syllabus. Although he was articulate, he was not cut out for taking these exams and achieved a shockingly low level in his KS3 test; in fact, he had regressed academically since primary school. The effect of the tests on him had been hugely damaging, demoralising him to such an extent that he felt there was no point ever trying at school.

I felt I had failed: I did manager to foster a love of reading but only at the cost of his exam results. Ultimately, Liam felt that his new-found love of reading was disconnected from everything he was doing in school.

Maths teachers report more or less the same problem: over-tested and demodulated children are not ready for secondary maths in the way they were before the tests were introduced.

The Key Stage 1 and 2 tests are to be retained. Yet most teachers know that this is where the rot starts: primary schools are obliged to brainwash their charges with test papers in order to keep their school's position high on the league tables.

This is not to say that schoolteachers have an easy life, handing out test papers and asking the pupils to get on with the work in silence. Teaching for SATs can be extremely difficult. Recently, the tests at all levels have become even more fiddly – and boring.

The English Key Stage 3 test, for which I have prepared pupils, follows a very set format: a reading paper, a writing paper and a Shakespeare paper. At a glance, it looks quite easy to teach. With Shakespeare, for instance, it benefits the teacher not to read the whole play, because only two scenes are tested; it is far more effective simply to show pupils the film and then drill them into understanding the two scenes set for the exam.

But the truth is that teaching even fairly short and easy set texts is a complicated affair. Because whatever you are teaching has to conform to set guidelines, guidelines which require that teachers teach every lesson to 'learning objectives'. At the beginning of each lesson the teacher writes at least one learning objective on the board, requiring pupils to copy it down in their books and focus on that particular concept throughout the lesson.

The response of one of my recent pupils, Leroy, sums up the attitude of many children. 'I've spent years copying this off the board and it makes me feel like a robot,' he told me. 'It's always just "targets". Copy this, copy that. Do this, do that. When are we ever going to do something we want to do?'

Leroy was a clever boy, but he messed around a lot during my Year 9 classes. In consequence, he achieved only an average Level 5 Sat, setting him up to achieve similarly undistinguished GCSEs. He should have gone on to do A-levels but didn't because he disliked school so much. In my opinion the exam system was entirely to blame for his dropping out.

Another pupil, Nicole, who was aged 13, once looked up at me at the end of the lesson and said that her hand was hurting from so much writing. 'This is all I do in every lesson, just fill in worksheets, but I never know what's important about any of this. Will I need any of this when I go to work?' she asked with sad resignation.

Nicole was a dutiful student and attained top marks in her SATs, but told me that she forgot everything she had learned a few weeks after the tests. It was an exaggeration, but it illustrated another problem with the tests: pupils didn't see that any of the skills they learned could be transferred to any other sphere.

The SATs foster the belief among our students that school is something abstract from the world beyond the classroom, existing in its own tortuous bubble.

Why then, if I hate them so much, do I feel apprehensive about the demise of the Key Stage 3 tests? Needless to say, the scrapping of the tests for 14-year-olds does not mean the scrapping of league tables or the measures that make teachers accountable for their pupils' results. So, while much is uncertain, it may be that teachers are scrutinised even *more* closely. The Department for Children, Schools and Families is piloting 'stage not age' tests, which are rather like music exams – tests that are taken when the pupil is ready to take them.

Apparently, these exams will assess pupils' knowledge and understanding of the new National Curriculum, which, worryingly, looks even worse than its predecessor in its use of ambiguous jargon.

Will the government never learn? What teachers, pupils and parents need are clear, concise guidelines that give them goals to work towards while still allowing them the freedom to teach.

All the SATs should be abolished now and replaced with simple, sensible tests.

## The big picture
By the time he or she finishes school, your child will have completed a whole battery of tests, assessments and exams. The bare bones of them are laid out in the chart overleaf.

| Age | Stage | Year | Assessment |
|------|--------|--------|-------------|
| 3-4 | Early Years Foundation Stage | | |
| 4-5 | | Reception | |
| 5-6 | Key Stage 1 | Year 1 | |
| 6-7 | | Year 2 | Teacher assessments in English, maths and science |
| 7-8 | Key Stage 2 | Year 3 | |
| 8-9 | | Year 4 | |
| 9-10 | | Year 5 | |
| 10-11 | Key Stage 3 | Year 6 | National tests and teacher assessments in English, maths and science |
| 11-12 | | Year 7 | |
| 12-13 | | Year 8 | Ongoing teacher assessments |
| 13-14 | | Year 9 | Teacher assessments in English, maths and science and the other foundation subjects |
| 14-15 | Key Stage 4 | Year 10 | Some children take GCSEs |
| 15-16 | | Year 11 | Most children take GCSEs or other national qualifications |

## Predicting your child's GCSE grades

A very useful thing to know is that you can roughly predict your child's GCSE scores when they are seven. Obviously, these predictions are not totally accurate; numerous factors may make your child far exceed expectations – or do the reverse. It is worth really knowing about this because you will be able to keep a good eye on your child's progress every year by looking at the Teacher Assessment Levels he or she is being given.

The basic rule is: a child should go up 2 Levels with each Key Stage. As explained in the chart above there are three 'levels' within a level: **a** which is top of the level, **b** which is middle and **c** which is bottom.

To give you an example: at Key Stage 1 a child with Level 2b should attain a Level 4b at Key Stage 2. At Key Stage 3 this pupil should be attaining a Level 6b, and at Key Stage 4, should attain a middling B grade at GCSE.

Your school will have 'added value' to your child if they exceed these grades at any stage. In other words, if the child above had attained an A grade at GCSE then the school would have *added the value* of a whole grade, giving the school a +1 value-added rating for that child. Schools that add value at the top end – that take for example a Level 5 student at 11 years old, and manage to get the child to attain a top scoring A* grade at GCSE – are doing a brilliant job. It is very difficult to do; it is a lot easier to add value when a child enters the school at a very low level of attainment.

## How can I predict my child's GCSE grade when they are seven?

The Key Stage 1 test is what is known as a Baseline Assessment which enables teachers to predict what children might achieve later on: it is the starting score or 'baseline' score from which all other scores are predicted and measured against. Obviously, if the Baseline Assessment is wrong, then all the subsequent predicted scores will be wrong. Nevertheless, the Key Stage 1 test is surprisingly accurate and you can get a good idea about what your child might achieve later on from it.

Have a look at the chart below and see if you get the hang of predicting GCSE grades.

| Key Stage | Level/grade | Predicted GCSE score based on this Level | Value-added + 1 |
|-----------|-------------|------------------------------------------|-----------------|
| Key Stage 1 | Level 2b) | Mid-level B grade: Bb | Mid-level A grade. |
| Key Stage 1 | Level 3a) | Top-level A grade: A*a | Exceptional performance at GCSE comment. |
| Key Stage 2 | Level 4b) | Mid-level B grade: Bb | Mid-level A grade: Ab |
| Key Stage 2 | Level 3b) | Mid-level C grade: Cb | Mid-level B grade: Bb |
| Key Stage 3 | Level 6c) | Low-level B grade: Bc | Low-level A grade: Ac |

## Key Stage 1 assessments

The Key Stage 1 assessment is one of the most important assessments he or she will ever take. This is taken at the end of Key Stage 1, when your child is aged seven. The tasks and tests cover:

- Reading
- Writing (including handwriting and spelling)
- Maths

The tasks and tests, lasting for less than three hours altogether, can be taken at a time when the school chooses. The results are not reported separately but are used to help the teacher assess your child's work – teacher assessment plays a big part too. These assessments for seven-year-olds cover:

- Reading
- Writing
- Speaking and listening
- Maths
- Science

By the age of seven, most children are expected to achieve level 2. It's not a test you should get your child in a panic about, it is purely there to establishment a 'benchmark' or 'baseline' by which your child's progress can be measured during the rest of school.

**Key Stage 2 assessments**
The heat is really on by Year 6 in many primary schools. You see, primary schools are largely judged on their Key Stage 2 test scores – and, as a result, can get very anxious about them. The best primary schools try and give their children a broad and balanced curriculum, making learning fun and interactive. The worst primary schools fill the whole of Year 6 with practice tests in English, Maths and Science; this is generally very boring for the pupils and engenders a fevered atmosphere that can make both pupils and teachers tense, snappy and very unhappy. The tests are very flawed at the moment; they encourage children to be very reductive in their reading of texts and, even worse, encourage teachers to give children little gobbets of text which are analysed to death, rather than to read whole books with their classes. By Year 6, pupils should be reading great novels by the likes of Michael Morpurgo, JK Rowling, Philip Pullman,

Malorie Blackman, not furrowing their brows over reductive test papers.

Key Stage 2 tests for 11-year-olds cover:

- English – reading, writing (including handwriting) and spelling
- Maths – including mental arithmetic
- Science (although at the time of writing, it has been ruled that these may be scrapped)

These tests are taken on set days in mid-May, and last less than five-and-a-half hours altogether.

By the age of 11, most children are expected to achieve level 4. But here again the 'levelling' that your child gets in the test may not be accurate. You should look at the other scores and marks they have achieved to get a real sense of where they are at. I have come across far too many parents who actually believe that because their child has got a Level 5 in the SATs he or she is a genius. Often they have ignored the far more accurate 'Teacher Assessment' levels, which I have found are often lower than the test scores. The test scores frequently engender dangerous complacency. I have taught far too many pupils with Level 5s in English at Key Stage 2 who think they are the bees knees and don't have to work. They've gone on to get disappointing GCSE results. Any pupil getting a Level 5 *should* attain an A grade in their GCSE. But the complacent pupils I've taught have sometimes scraped C and B grades, never quite fulfilling their promise because they've felt they can 'coast'.

For sample papers log onto these websites run by Woodlands Junior School in Kent and St Josephs in Pickering. A word of warning, though: SATs may well be changing soon so don't bank on the format of the test staying the same.

**Sample English, maths and science papers:** http://www.st

josephs-pickering.n-yorks.sch.uk/past_test_papers.htm

**Sample maths papers:** http://www.woodlands-junior.kent.sch.uk/maths/sats/index.html

**Sample science papers:** http://www.woodlands-junior.kent.sch.uk/revision/Science/index.html


### Can my child fail his/her Key Stage tests?

No! Your child can't fail the test, but he or she can 'under-achieve' – meaning that they either don't fulfil the expectations the school has of him or her or they don't attain the score predicted by their previous test scores. In which case, you need to ask that your child is given an Individual Action Plan for improvement.


### Will my child's secondary school be decided by their Key Stage test results?

No! The Key Stage tests are not used to select pupils for their next school. They are there purely to inform you and the school about how he or she is getting on. They help teachers find out the strength and weaknesses of pupils and enable them to work on them in the following year.


### Is the Key Stage 2 test taken by children at 11 years old the same as the 11-plus?

No! The 11-plus is taken by children who live in areas where there are grammar schools. Grammar schools are the only state schools allowed to select their intake purely on the basis of academic ability.

There is a large industry built around the 11-plus. If you are not careful, you could spend thousands of pounds paying for sample papers and tutors. This is, quite frankly, outrageous and exploitative. There is one website campaigning for free resources. It is: http://www.chuckra.co.uk/educational/ and gives away free resources to help with the taking of the tests.

My advice is: DON'T WASTE MONEY ON TESTS OR TUTORS! Your child's school should be educating them, not you or their tutors.

The main thing to bear in mind is that your child should be:

- Reading for pleasure
- Writing fluently and accurately
- Speaking and listening confidently

If he or she is, then they will do well no matter what school they go to.


### Key Stage 3 teacher assessments

The abolition of Key Stage 3 tests just may, as I have said, actually improve the education of many pupils. I am breathing a sigh of relief because now all my energies will be devoted to improving my pupils' English skills, not teaching them to tick the right boxes. Now pupils will need to actually pay attention to their teachers and not the wretched revision guides that dominated their lives during the year.

The Key Stage 3 teacher assessment for 14-year-olds covers:

- English
- Maths
- Science
- History
- Geography
- Modern foreign languages
- Design and technology
- Information and Communication Technology (ICT)
- Art and design

- Music
- Physical education
- Citizenship
- Religious education

The best schools will doubtless hold end-of-year exams and look at their pupils' performance in them, but will also assess them on what they have done in class and for homework. The 'Teacher Assessment' grades should be much more accurate than the Key Stage results.

By the age of 14, most children are expected to achieve level 6s in most of their subjects, particularly the 'core', which are English, maths and science. Year 9 is really the year when your child should be moving onto studying 'analytically': writing critically in English, dealing with more complicated algebra in maths, learning in depth about chemistry, physics and biology in science.

## Qualification soup: GCSEs, Entry Level qualifications, vocational courses

GCSE stands for General Certificate of Secondary Education and are still, despite their detractors, the main and most respected qualifications for 16-year-olds; generally they are taught over two years in Years 10 and 11. The number of GCSEs your child can take is huge: there are more than 45 academic subjects available and various 'applied' subjects, which are all 'work-related'. There are currently eight 'applied' GCSEs:

- Applied art and design
- Applied business
- Applied ICT
- Applied science
- Engineering
- Health and social care

- Leisure and tourism
- Manufacturing

GCSEs can also be taken as short courses, which are the equivalent of half a GCSE and take a year to complete, and cover half the material. They are very useful if your child wants to take an extra foreign language.

## A brief note on point scores and qualifications

For all recognised qualifications at all key stages, the Department for Children, Schools and Families allocates points. Every National Curriculum level your child achieves is converted into points. Usually, the total points for all pupils are averaged and the DCSF then works out the average point score for pupils at each school. The point score information is there not least to enable the DCSF to see whether a school is adding value to pupils at the different key stages.

Now that all qualifications are part of the point score system, it enables useful comparisons. For example, you can compare a BTEC qualification with an A Level qualification in terms of the points awarded; a Distinction in the BTEC National Award is worth 270 points, as is an A Level Grade A. It is not an entirely fail-safe system – a vocational award which consists of a great deal of course work is *not* equivalent to an A-level in Physics, whatever the points system might suggest. However, this is the system in place – and in all likelihood it will stay for years to come.

## Tiers and grades at GCSE

In some subjects, such as history, music and art and design, everybody sits exactly the same exam paper. In some subjects, like English, science, most foreign languages and maths, pupils have a choice of different 'tiers':

- The *foundation tier* assesses grades G to C
- The *higher tier* assesses grades D to A*

**Assessment**

Most of the assessment at GCSE takes place on written exams, although in some subjects there is coursework. Some GCSEs such as science GCSEs, consist of 'units': exams are taken at the end of each unit.

GCSEs are marked numerically and then the 'raw marks' are converted into grades.

**Is it important what my child chooses to do for GCSE?**

Yes, it is! As has been said before, the more academic universities want to see pupils gaining top grades in the following subjects:

- English
- English literature
- Maths
- Science (Science can be taken as a single GCSE, a 'dual award' GCSE, or, for the most able students, as three separate subjects. Doing separate papers in biology, physics, and chemistry is very important if your child is considering medicine at university)
- A modern foreign language
- A humanities-based subject such as religious education, history or geography

**What will my child have to study to GCSE level?**

- English Language (English Literature is increasingly becoming an 'option' in school)

- Maths
- Science

(These can be taken as entry level qualifications – very simple exams for pupils who can't cope with the mainstream qualifications.)

There are some other subjects that you have to study, but may not lead to exams:

- Careers education
- Citizenship
- Information and communication technology (ICT)
- Physical education (PE)
- Religious studies
- Sex and relationships education
- Work-related learning

Some schools have other compulsory subjects: more academic schools usually insist upon pupils doing a modern foreign language and a humanities subject such as history or geography.

### What's voluntary?

Your school must provide pupils with at least ONE of the following 'entitlement' areas, which every child has the right to study:

- Arts – which includes art and design, music, drama and media arts
- Design and Technology
- Humanities – Geography and History
- Modern Foreign Languages

Other options can typically include:

- Business studies
- Engineering

- Health and Social Care
- Leisure and Tourism
- Skills for working life
- Life skills
- Manufacturing
- Social Sciences

These subjects may have different names at your child's school.


## Key and Functional Skills

Since the mid-1990s the government has worried that pupils still aren't learning the basics while studying for their GCSEs, so it has introduced both 'Key and Functional Skills', which aim to teach:

- Communication
- Working with others
- Problem solving
- Number skills

Language, mathematics and ICT skills ('Functional Skills') will become part of all qualifications, including GCSEs, Diplomas and Apprenticeships. Functional Skills will also be available as stand-alone qualifications.

Whether they are taken seriously as qualifications remains to be seen: the last time the government tried to introduce Key Skills at A Level it was a miserable and extremely costly failure and had to be abandoned. Will it have learnt from mistakes?

My feeling is that it might have done: the new Key and Functional Skills tests will be mostly conducted online and marked more precisely than the ridiculous Key Skills of yesteryear. Having seen some trial tests, I approve: the 'Language' tests actually see whether pupils know how to punctuate – which is more than the current English GCSE does.

**Should my child consider doing a vocational qualification?**
Some schools, but not all, offer vocational qualifications, BTEC and OCR Nationals, which give you skills directly related to the world of work. They are well worth considering if your child is really not at ease with the academic subjects.

Many BTEC and OCR Nationals have a 'work experience' component, and are designed with the co-operation of the industry or sector they relate to. The qualifications offer a mix of theory and practice; they can take the form of a technical certificate, or can form the key components of an Apprenticeship.

An 'Apprenticeship' is essentially 'on the job' training, which requires no qualifications, although some require A*-C grades in maths and English. There are more than 180 Apprenticeships available across more than 80 industry sectors. They include accountancy, business administration, construction, engineering, manufacturing and many more.

The NVQ (National Vocational Qualification) is a 'competence-based' qualification, which means instead of learning theories and concepts, pupils primarily learn how to be 'competent' in the relevant areas; the qualification spells out very clearly what the learner is expected to do. It is very hands-on, designed to prepare someone for the world of work in a specific area. (NVQs are assessed at levels 1 to 5 on the National Qualifications Framework – see below.)

Because they are so vocational, it is mainly adults who do NVQs, although they are available as an option for young people too. Usually it is only the most disaffected young students who do take them up, however. When a school has run out of ideas about how to engage a troubled, switched-off pupil, they might try a Young Apprenticeship scheme, tying it in with a NVQ in a relevant area. The wonderful thing about NVQs is the sheer range of subjects that can be covered. You name it and it's got a course: there are over 1300 different NVQs to choose from. They are available mostly in the commercial sectors and include courses based around:

- Business and management
- Sales, marketing and distribution
- Health care
- Food, catering and leisure services
- Construction and property
- Manufacturing, production and engineering

These are highly regarded qualifications and if you think that your child is really finding school tough when they are 14+, then you should seriously consider putting him or her on a Young Apprenticeship. For more information, contact the Careers Advice helpline: 0800 100 900 or http://careersadvice.direct.gov.uk/

**Should my child do one of these new Diplomas?**
The Diploma Scheme has had a terrible press so far because its introduction has been so disorganised. Nevertheless, if the teething problems are solved, then it could be an exciting qualification. Unlike the NVQ, which is primarily aimed at adults, the Diploma is specifically aimed at 14- to 19-year-olds. The government claims it is 'a practical, hands-on way of gaining the knowledge and skills you need for college, university or work.'

There's no doubt in my mind that the traditional universities will look warily at the Diploma. Nevertheless, the newer ones, particularly those involved in the Diploma's set-up and implementation, may well be much keener.

My advice is the same as for the NVQs. Use the Diploma as a 'last resort'; if all the other academic subjects are really failing to motivate and engage your child, you have nothing to lose. Rather than failing their GCSEs, they will, in all likelihood, 'pass' the new Diploma.

### Getting a good mix

The crucial thing is to give your child a chance to do subjects that inspire them. The rule should be: they should go with their passions. The world is changing so fast that we just don't know what will be valued in ten years time. But there's no doubt that fired-up, enthusiastic young people will thrive, whatever the subjects they've studied.

### Why do I have to understand the National Qualifications Framework?

The National Qualifications Framework shows you what qualifications are 'worth'. It sets out the level at which a qualification can be recognised in England, Northern Ireland and Wales, and shows you where your child might go next. Understanding it will help give you a 'road map' of where your child is heading.

# Assessment

| NQF level | Examples of qualifictaions | What they give you |
|---|---|---|
| Entry | - Entry level certificates<br>- Skills for Life at entry level | - basic knowledge and skills<br>- ability to apply learning in everyday situations<br>- not geared towards specific occupations |
| 1 | - GCSEs grades D-G<br>- BTEC Introductory Diplomas and Certificates<br>- OCR Nationals<br>- Key Skills level 1<br>- NVQs<br>- Skills for Life | - basic knowledge and skills<br>- ability to apply learning with guidance or supervision<br>- may be linked to job competence |
| 2 | - GCSEs grades A*-C<br>- BTEC First Diplomas and Certificates<br>- OCR Nationals<br>- Key Skills level 2<br>- NVQs<br>- Skills for Life | - good knowledge and understanding of a subject<br>- ability to perform variety of tasks with some guidance or supervision<br>- appropriate for many job roles |
| 3 | - A levels<br>- Advanced Extension Awards<br>- GCE in applied subjects<br>- International Baccalaureate<br>- Key Skills level 3<br>- NVQs<br>- BTEC Diplomas, Certificates and Awards<br>- BTEC Nationals<br>- OCR Nationals | - ability to gain or apply a range of knowledge, skills and understanding, at a detailed level<br>- appropriate if you plan to go to university, work independently, or (in some cases) supervise and train others in their field of work |
| 4 | - Key Skills level 4<br>- NVQs<br>- BTEC Professional Diplomas, Certificates and Awards | - specialist learning, involving detailed analysis of a high level of information and knowledge in an area of work or study<br>- appropriate for people working in technical and professional jobs, and/or managing and developing others |

| NQF level | Examples of qualifictaions | What they give you |
|---|---|---|
| 5 | - Higher National Certificates and Higher National Diplomas<br>- NVQs<br>- BTEC Professional Diplomas, Certificates and Awards | - ability to increase the depth of knowledge and understanding of an area of work or study, so you can respond to complex problems and situations<br>- involves high level of work expertise and competence in managing and training others<br>- appropriate for people working as higher grade technicians, professionals or managers |
| 6 | - National Diploma in Professional Production Skills<br>- BTEC Advanced Professional Diplomas, Certificates and Awards<br>- Diploma in Translation<br>- BTEC Advanced Professional Diplomas, Certificates and Awards<br>- specialist awards | - a specialist, high-level knowledge of an area of work or study, to enable you to use your own ideas and research in response to complex problems and situations<br>- appropriate for people working as knowledge-based professionals or in professional management positions |
| 7 | - Diploma in Translation<br>- BTEC Advanced Professional Diplomas, Certificates and Awards | - highly developed and complex levels of knowledge, enabling you to develop original responses to complicated and unpredictable problems and situations<br>- appropriate for senior professionals and managers |
| 8 | - specialist awards | - opportunity to develop new and creative approaches that extend or redefine existing knowledge or professional practice<br>- appropriate for leading experts or practitioners in a particular field |

The government now also has a good up-to-date web-based service at http://www.direct.gov.uk/en/EducationAndLearning/index.htm It is well worth exploring this website to gain the latest information as information can often change.

## Why finding out your child's exam boards for the different subjects is vital

The most useful thing you could do to help your child with their GCSEs is find out what exam board they are studying for each subject and then guide them to the sample assessment material, the exam papers and the syllabi on the relevant website.

Even though I am always telling my pupils which exam board we are with, they often don't take in the information. The exam board's websites are INCREDIBLY USEFUL! Full of materials, tips, advice, and help. Don't waste your money on revision guides, check them out.

There are five exam boards that offer GCSE qualifications:

- Assessment and Qualifications Alliance http://www.aqa.org.uk

- Northern Ireland Council for the Curriculum, Examinations and Assessments http://www.ccea.org.uk

- Edexcel http://www.examzone.co.uk and http://www.edexcel.org.uk

- Oxford, Cambridge and RSA Examinations http://www.ocr.org.uk

- Welsh Joint Education Committee http://www.wjec.co.uk

## Regulatory authorities

There are three regulatory authorities that oversee what exam boards do. As regulators, it's their job to monitor standards and make sure that GCSEs don't get harder or easier each year, so that pupils get a fair deal. Or at least that's what they say; too often these quangos are the incompetent puppets of their political masters.

- In England: (Qualifications and Curriculum Authority) http://www.qca.org.uk

- In Wales: (Department for Education, Lifelong Learning and Skills)http://www.wales.gov.uk
- In Northern Ireland: (Council for the Curriculum, Examinations and Assessments) http://www.ccea.org.uk

## How do I motivate my child to do well in exams?

**Do:**

Talk positively with your child about their school work. This is the simplest and most important rule, but perhaps the most difficult to do. It is very easy to slip into a negative cycle and end up nagging or interrogating.

Use the internet to help become more enthusiastic about subjects they don't like. Google subjects they're finding difficult and get them to look at some engaging, relevant websites. Check out the videos for the subject on You Tube.com. Sign up for a Google account (www.google.co.uk/accounts) and get them to put notes and links on Google docs or set up a blog.

Help your child get organised. Help your child tidy their room and put their work into the relevant folders and files. Make it clear you won't always be helping them but you will now because it's important to get them on the right track. Use posters and calendars to help them be organised.

Get them a mentor; reading the article below should convince you that mentoring is a sure-fire way of helping a child who is struggling.

Use 'points' to set up a 'positive' reward system. Trying to bribe children with ONE big prize at the end of the year or after some good results rarely works: the prize becomes the sole motivation, not the work. However, if you agree to give points regularly for good work, which could then be added up to get a prize, this will work more effectively. For example, giving a point for good homework or wider reading and agreeing that 200 points gains a 'final reward' sets up a 'virtuous circle' of positive comments and approbation.

## Don't:
Nag or shout or scream or threaten. It might work in the short term, but in the long term, it always backfires and demotivates.

Push your child too hard.

Have low expectations. Expect the best and you may well get it.

Have impossibly high standards where only the very top is good enough.

# Conclusion

*I forget what I was taught.*
*I only remember what I have learnt.* **Patrick White**

**What are the key lessons of this book?**

1  Be consistent: have consistent rules, routines, and attitudes.

2  Stimulate your children.

3  Discuss things.

4  Be positive and open-minded about learning.

5  Aim high.

6  Get involved with your child's school.

Desforges' research shows pretty conclusively that if you get these things right, then it ultimately doesn't matter where your child goes to school.

That said, life is going to be a hell of a lot easier if you can get your child into a good school. The key points to remember are:

- Do your research first. Look at the league tables and Ofsted reports.

- Visit the school and ask searching questions. Remember the Holy Grail is finding a good headteacher and good teachers! Don't be prejudiced. Some of the best schools now are inner-city schools that were failing a decade ago.

- If you want your child to go to the school make sure you fill in the forms correctly. You must meet the 'admissions criteria'. If your child doesn't get in and you can make a case, appeal!

Once your child is at school, you should try and get involved in school life. If you are not happy with the teaching or if your child is unhappy, don't suffer in silence. Parents have a lot of rights now. You have a right for your child to be put on an 'Individual Action Plan' which will improve their achievement.

If your child is struggling with the work, then make sure he or she is assessed to see if he has Special Educational Needs. If he is finding the work too easy, ask for him to be put on the Gifted and Talented register and given work to stretch him. Use the full range of facilities on offer: ask for extra mentoring, extra classes, or teach him yourself if necessary. Do remember that education is much more than the narrow academic curriculum. Cooking with your child, discussing the news and talking about difficult issues like sex, relationships and drugs is education too! Probably the most important education your child will have.

If your child is being bullied, make sure the school investigate the issue thoroughly. Schools are much better at doing this now. Also use some of my guidelines in the chapter on bullying to help your child deal with it himself.

Finally, remember that learning doesn't stop at school. Your child should enjoy the process and have fun. If he or she isn't, then you need to look hard at yourself, your child's school and his or her life. Re-evaluate it. Take stock. Think of ways he or she could enjoy learning more. It is only when a child enjoys the process of learning that the real education begins.

# Select reading

*Could Do Better: Help Your Kid Shine at School* by Phil Beadle (Doubleday, 2007). This is a wonderful book, jam-packed with lively ideas about how to enthuse and motivate your child at home. Highly recommended and a real antidote to the Janis-Norton book of the same title.

*What every parent should know...before their child goes to secondary school* by Jane Bidder (White Ladder Press, 2007). A clear, no-nonsense guide that explains the new legislation and its impact upon parents. The best bits are the short quotes from parents, which are really illuminating. Of the many parent guides I read in the course of researching this book, I found this was the one I had most sympathy with.

*The School I'd Like – Children and Young People's Reflections on an Education for the 21st Century* by Catherine Burke and Ian Grosvenor (Routledge, 2003). This is a fascinating little book full of children's accounts of the school they'd like in the 21st century. It is full of children's poems, essays, pictures and plans, together with the authors' comments on them. There is an excellent chapter on 'Survival', which really paints a truthful portrait of life in school at the moment.

*Could Do Better...How Parents Can Help Their Children Succeed at School* by Noel Janis-Norton (Barrington Stoke, 2005). I found this a depressing book because it is really about 'training' your child to learn large chunks of information, training them to pass spelling tests, to improve their memory, to improve their concentration.

The tone is feverish, almost panic-stricken at points. Nevertheless, it is useful because it will give you an insight into what some pushy parents will be doing with their children. The book fails to recognise the intrinsic joy of learning and reduces it to a series of mechanical exercises. While paying lip-service to enthusing and motivating your child, the overall approach in it appears to be about fostering blind obedience.

*The Reading Bug; and how you can help your child to catch it* by Paul Jennings (Penguin, 2004). Jennings' book is a perfect antidote to the above: a book which is primarily about encouraging reading by motivating, not frightening, your child to read.

*The Parent/Child Game – The Proven Key to a Happier Family* by Sue Jenner (Bloomsbury, 2008). Clinical psychologist Jenner makes an important distinction between child-centred and child -directive parenting. The former involves praise, smiling, ignoring minor naughtiness, asking to play, positive touching and imitation, while the latter is about criticism, the 'negative face' – disapproving looks etc, saying 'no', commands, negative touch and teaching. No prizes for guessing what she advocates. This is a persuasive and important book which reveals the importance of 'enjoying' being a parent.

*Bullying – Brilliant ideas for keeping your child safe and happy* by Dr Sabina Dosani (Infinite Ideas, 2008). This is the most parent-friendly book on bullying I have read because of its tone and approach: it contains many, many different ideas about how to solve bullying problems without taking a prescriptive approach. It encourages parents to explore different avenues as well as covering the main research that has been conducted int this area. Highly recommended.

*May Contain Nuts* by John O'Farrell (Transworld, 2006). A hilarious novel about a pushy parent in South London who learns to love the state schooling system. The uptight mum is so anxious at one point that she disguises herself as a school child and sits an exam!

*Happy Families: how to make one, how to keep one* by Bill Lucas, with clinical psychologist Dr Stephen Briers (BBC Books, 2000). This is a more general book about being a good parent, but so much of its advice is applicable to schools. There is a MUST-READ comic strip section in the middle about the different parenting styles.

*One Out Of Ten* by Peter Hyman (Vintage, 2005). This is definitely the most fascinating recent book on the role politics plays in education. It is written by a former speech writer for Tony Blair who became a teacher in one of the roughest comprehensives in London. Ignore all the slavish praise of Tony, and you'll find an eye-opening book full of great advice and insight. It is a very handy guide for any parent who sends their child to an inner-city school.

*Learning In Tandem – involving parents in their children's education* by Ruth Merttens, Alan Newland and Susie Webb (Scholastic, 1996). This book contains the best summaries of the theories of 'learning' that have informed teaching in recent years, looking at the ways in which parents can improve their children's learning in the classroom.

# Useful Websites

Important rule: Never part with your money when looking for school advice on the internet. You can get great free advice if you look in the right places. The best place to start is The Advisory Service for Education – see below.

**The BBC website** for schools is also pretty good and much more interactive, if a little bland at times: http://www.bbc.co.uk/schools/parents

For advice on **books** and **reading** look at the Booktrust website: http://www.booktrust.org.uk or the Literacy Trust website: http://www.literacytrust.org.uk

For help dealing with **bullying:** http://www.bullying.co.uk http://www.kidscape.org.uk http://www.teachernet.gov.uk/wholeschool/behaviour/tacklingbullying

For help on most **matters connected with children**: http://www.ncb.org.uk/Page.asp Founded in 1963, the National Children's Bureau (NCB) is a charitable organisation that acts as an umbrella body for organisations working with children and young people in England & Northern Ireland. Through working in partnership, sharing knowledge, resources and services they have created a powerful, authoritative and influential voice to improve the lives of children and young people.

For serious **complaints** which have not been dealt with by the governing body, go to the Local Ombudsman: http://www.lgo.org.uk or for serious complaints about the admissions criteria of a school your child hasn't got into go to the School's Adjudicator: http://www.schoolsadjudicator.gov.uk

For **more about me**, my journalism, my blog, my teaching materials, my advice for parents: http://www.francisgilbert.co.uk

For **government information** (and propaganda) about state schools: http://www.dcsf.gov.uk. For Wales: http://new.wales.gov.uk/topics/educationandskills/?lang=en. This site is massive and includes links to many other important sites. It is easy to get lost in. You should look at the parents' centre site (see below) before trawling through this one in detail. For information on **government grants** or Educational Maintenance Allowance for Sixth Formers: http://ema.direct.gov.uk

For examination syllabi and past exam questions, check the wonderful websites of the **examination boards**. They are choc-full of past examination papers for GCSE and A Level and will save you a fortune in revision guides. But before you do make doubly sure you know what syllabus your child is following. For AQA: http://www.aqa.org.uk, Edexcel: http://www.edexcel.org.uk, OCR: http://www.ocr.org.uk, Welsh Joint Education Committee: http://www.wjec.co.uk, Northern Ireland Council for the Curriculum, Examinations and Assessments: http://www.ccea.org.uk. Remember a syllabus (an outline of what topics must be covered) for a course is now called a 'Specification' and they can all be downloaded very quickly from these sites.

For information on children who are **gifted and talented**: http://www.nagcbritain.org.uk

For **impartial schools' advice**, the charity **The Advisory Centre for Education** is worth a look: http://www.ace-ed.org.uk. It is particularly good if you have a specific problem that requires legal advice while the FAQ section answers most common queries about choosing schools, bullying, SEN.

For information on state and independent schools:

http://www.goodschoolsguide.co.uk

*The Good Schools' Guide* is published as a book every year with detailed updated information on the top schools in the country. Subscribing to their advisory service and buying the book is a waste of money: contact **The Advisory Centre for Education** for free advice.

For parents who are or are interested in becoming **governors**, look at: http://www.governornet.co.uk, http://www.sgoss.org.uk /home/individuals.htm. is a one-stop-shop for school governors.

For information about **healthy eating**: http://www.eatwell.gov.uk http://www.schoolfoodtrust.org.uk

For information on **home schooling**: http://www.education-otherwise.org

For **mentoring** advice: http://www.standards.dfes.gov.uk/learn-ingmentors or the Mentoring and Befriending Foundation have lots to offer: http://www.mandbf.org.uk

For information about the **National Curriculum**: http://cur-riculum.qca.org.uk

For the most recent **Ofsted** reports on your child's school: http:// www.ofsted.gov.uk or Estyn, the office of Her Majesty's Inspectorate for Education and Training in Wales: http://www.estyn. gov.uk/home.asp

To find **information on any state school**, and for school profiles (schools' annual reports): http://schoolsfinder.direct.gov.uk

For more **parents' information on schools**: http://www.par-entscentre.gov.uk. This is an excellent site which contains a whole host of other contacts and links to their publications, which are clearly and accurately written. CASE (The Campaign For State Education) is also excellent on all issues but definitely stridently anti-selection: http://www.campaignforstateeducation.org.uk

For **general guidance on parenting**: http://www.youngminds. org.uk . *Young Minds* on 0800 018 2138 – a parents' information service providing confidential advice for any adult concerned about the mental health or emotional well-being of a child or young person. Parentline Plus helpline on 0808 800 2222 – provides help and information for anyone caring for children: http://www.parentlineplus.org.uk. Parentline Plus also runs a great site for **parents with teenagers**: http://www.gotateenager. org.uk

*Child Line* on 0800 1111 – offers help to young people in trouble or danger: http://www.childline.org.uk/Pages/default.aspx

Great **advice for mothers** can be found on: http://www.net-mums.com/home/home Once you have registered on your local site you can access details for all kinds of local resources, from child-friendly cafes to childminders. Mumsnet (www.mumsnet. com) is also an excellent site for discussion and tip-swapping.

**Advice for fathers**: the Fatherhood institute doesn't look as much fun, but it's certainly an informative site: http://www.fatherhoo-dinstitute.org. Its aims are: collating the research on fatherhood; helping shape the government's family policy; influencing the public debate on fathers; training family services to be father-inclusive. For a more informal approach, check out: http://www. dadtalk.co.uk/index.php

For **free legal advice**: http://www.childrenslegalcentre.com/ or http://www.communitylegaladvice.org.uk/index.jsp. More specialist advice about educational law can be found at:

http://www.educationlawassociation.org.uk/

For help with **lone parenting** look at Gingerbread: http://www.oneparentfamilies.org.uk/loneparents. The site is almost a one-stop shop for lone parents, giving advice on most issues: SEN, money, housing, divorce etc.

For **special needs** advice: http://www.csie.org.uk The Centre for Studies on Inclusive Education is a charity campaigning for and supporting children with special needs. For parents who have disabled children: http://www.cafamily.org.uk/index.php?section=861. For free advice on **appealing decisions made about special needs**: http://www.ipsea.org.uk

For help with **deaf children**: http://www.ndcs.org.uk. The National Children's Deaf Society supports children with any type of hearing difficulty. For getting help on enabling your child to join mainstream education: http://www.network81.org. Network 81 is a national network of parents working towards properly resourced inclusive education for children with special educational needs.

For getting help with **speech difficulties**: http://www.ican.org.uk/TalkingPoint/Home.aspx Lots of tips and advice on helping your child improve their speech as well as the offer of free assessments by professionals.

If you wish to **contest a decision** made about your child regarding Special Needs, look at: http://www.sendist.gov.uk/index.htm. The First Tier Tribunal for Special Educational Needs & Disability was set up by the Education Act 1993. It considers parents' appeals against the decisions of Local Authorities (LA's) about children's special educational needs if parents cannot reach agreement with the LA. The Tribunal is independent.

# Useful Websites

For information about **state education**: http://www.risetrust. org.uk. RISE reports have covered many issues of particular interest to parents e.g. class size, school reports, home-school agreements, parental involvement in OFSTED inspections, school complaints procedures, school admissions and the role of parent governor representatives.

For parents with children who are involved with or require the **social services**: http://www.frg.org.uk/

For **teachers** or **parents who are teachers**, or just parents who are interested in teaching, log onto: http://www.teachernet.gov. uk/. Check out Teachers' TV on digital TV as well. Many of the programmes are relevant to any parents who are interested in their child's education. The website has many of the programmes to download. I think it the one successful initiative the government has launched in recent years: http://www.teachers.tv/

# Glossary

**AD(H)D Attention Deficit (Hyperactivity) Disorder.** If you suspect your child has difficulty concentrating in lessons and is very restless much of the time, he or she may be suffering from this condition. Please read the SEN section on how to get your child assessed for this condition. For more information contact the National ADD Information and Support Service: http://www.addiss.co.uk or http://www.adders.org. These are both sites which will give you a whole host of information on the condition and further contact details.

**Autism spectrum disorders.** Autism is a neurological condition which makes it difficult for child to form relationships or communicate with others. At the mild end of the spectrum there is "Asperger's syndrome" which might cause a child to be uncommunicative and their behaviour eccentric and and at the other there is extreme autism which means a child will find it almost impossible to communicate properly with people. For more information log onto the website of the National Autism society: http://www.nas.org.uk.

**Admissions Authority.** Some types of schools – Voluntary- aided, Foundation and Trust schools – have their own admissions authorities because parents send their application direct to that individual school. Parents must NOT forget to apply through their Local Education Authority as well though. Some schools – Community and Voluntary-controlled – have their admissions controlled by the LEA. Parents can only apply for them through the LEA.

**Admissions Criteria.** It is vital that you read the criteria or list of rules that each school uses to select their pupils.

Voluntary-aided, foundation and trust schools can set their own admissions criteria. TOP TIP: Many parents work the system by making sure that they read the admissions criteria of their favoured schools very carefully and meet all the requirements.

**AS Level.** This stands for Advanced Supplementary Level, which is the first part of an A-Level which pupils usually take in Year 12.

**A2 Level.** The second year of A Level.

**Baseline Assessment.** This is the FIRST assessment made by a teacher during your child's first weeks at primary school. It is an important assessment to get right because your child performance in tests in future years will be measured against his performance in his baseline assessment. Children are assessed for Language and Literacy, Maths and Personal and Social Skills.

**BSP.** Behavioural Support Plan.

**BTECs.** Business and Technology Education Council.

**CAT.** Cognitive Ability Test (Produced by the National Foundation for Educational Research). This is essentially an IQ test which tests a child's reasoning skills with words, quantities and spatial patterns. Many schools use the test because it does not require much prior knowledge to achieve a good result. It is a very good predictor of natural intelligence as opposed to learned intelligence. TOP TIP: It is well worth knowing what your child's CATS score is. For more information: http://www.nfer-nelson.co.uk/education/resources/cat3/faqs.asp?css=1#faq1

**Catchment Area.** The area from which a school takes their pupils. The majority of admission authorities now give priority to children who live in an area around the school, but there may be other priorities though.

**Community School.** The LEA controls the admissions for these schools.

**CVA.** Context Value-Added. A new method Ofsted is using to measure the performance of schools. The CVA takes into account the social background of the pupils in measuring how well they have done. Fairly dodgy statistics in my view, but they are increasingly being used to make judgements about schools.

**County Schools.** The LEA controls admissions for these schools.

**CTC.** City Technology College.

**DCSF.** Department for Children, Schools and Families, the government department which supervises the running of schools throughout the country.

**Differentiation.** QCA defines this as: "The organisation of teaching programmes and methods specifically to suit the age, ability and aptitudes of specific children." TOP TIP: All state schools should "differentiate". This means that the work set should engage your child and help him learn. If the work isn't doing this, you should request an Individual Action Plan for your child.

**Dyslexia.** While many people argue about the precise meaning of this term, it is essentially a learning disability which affects reading skill. Persons with dyslexia may have difficulty remembering, recognizing, and/or reversing written letters, numbers, and words, might read backwards, and have poor handwriting. TOP TIP: for more information log onto http://www.dyslexiaaction.org.uk. This excellent site gives parents a full and accurate checklist of points in order to diagnose dyslexia. You could also read *The Secret Life of the Dyslexic Child – a practical guide for parents and educators* by Robert Frank, (Rodale, 2002) and *Day-to-Day Dyslexia in the Classroom – Second Edition* (2004) by Joy Pollock, Elizabeth Waller, and Rody Politt (Routledge 2004).

**Dyspraxia.** This is a severe difficulty in performing tasks requiring fine motor skills such as drawing or writing. TOP TIP read: *Dyspraxia, Developmental Co-ordination Disorder* by Dr Amanda Kirby (Souvenir Press, 2006). *Making Inclusion Work for Children With Dyspraxia – Practical Strategies For Teachers* (2004) by Gill Dixon and Lois M. Addy, (Routledge, 2004).

**EBD.** Emotional and Behavioural Difficulties.

**EAL.** English as an Additional Language.

**ESL.** English as a Second Language.

**Every Child Matters.** (As if they didn't before this legislation was passed!) This is a new government approach to the well-being of children and young people from birth to age 19. The Government's aim is for every child, whatever their background or their circumstances, to have the support they need to:
- Be healthy
- Stay safe
- Enjoy and achieve
- Make a positive contribution

- Achieve economic well-being

Website: http://www.everychildmatters.gov.uk. No one in the education field has got their head around what this new legislation means yet, but it appears to give parents many more rights than they had before. For example, it seems that if your child is being badly bullied, you may have recourse to law since he or she isn't "safe" at school. This is, as yet, untested in the courts.

**Exclusion.** The suspension or expulsion of a pupil from school for disciplinary reasons. TOP TIP: You can appeal against an exclusion if you think it is unfair by contacting the school governing body disciplinary committee.

**Extended schools.** The government is aiming for ALL state schools to become schools which open well beyond the normal school hours, with its premises being used for after-school clubs, parenting classes or anything else the wider community requires. TOP TIP: Always check your school's noticeboard for information about free classes etc.

**Feeder schools.** Some admissions authorities automatically accept pupils from specific primary schools. TOP TIP: always check the admissions criteria of your favoured schools a few years in advance.

**Foundation Schools.** These schools have the power to set their own admissions but are nominally run by the LEA.

**GCE. General Certificate of Education.** These are A-Levels by any other name. It is particularly important to bear this in mind when looking up syllabi on the internet. TOP TIP: Make sure your child chooses the right A Levels. As with A-Levels, certain vocational GCEs are not as respected asthe "gold standard" ones such as the Sciences, English Literature, Maths and Further Maths.

**GCSE. General Certificate of Secondary Education.** These replaced the old O Levels. TOP TIP: These are the most important your child will take. Make sure that they are taking the right GCSEs. Many top universities will expect their top students to have taken at least EIGHT respectable GCSEs (English, English Literature, Maths, Sciences – double or triple – a Humanities subject, a Modern Foreign Language) and achieved A*-A grades in most!

**Healthy Schools Initiative.** A multifaceted initiative aimed at improving the health of pupils and teachers. In particular, it has set strict guidelines for school dinners but has also asked schools to address a multitude of health issues, including encouraging students to make their own fresh food. TOP TIP: Find out if your school is abiding by the new regulations: http://www.healthyschools.gov.uk/

**HMI.** Her Majesty's Inspectors for schools. Otherwise known as Ofsted.

**HOF.** Head of Faculty. See Head of Department below.

**HOD.** Head of Department. Responsible for the academic standards in their subject. TOP TIP: See the relevant Head of Department if your child is struggling in a particular subject.

**Home-school agreements.** Every state school should have asked parents to sign a home-school agreement. The agreements aim to make parents aware of their responsibilities and the school's ethos and guidelines. TOP TIP: Hold your school to account if the school has promised to mark and assess work regularly but has failed to do so.

**HOY.** Head of Year: these crucial teachers, usually found in secondary schools, are responsible for overseeing the behaviour and learning in their year group. TOP TIP: See the Head of Year if there is a behavioural issue such as bullying, or a problem with the quality of teaching.

**IAP or Individual Action Plan.** Every child is entitled to have an Individual Action Plan that will help him or her learn in the most effective way. TOP TIP: You are entitled to have this plan "personalised" to meet your child's specific learning styles. See http://www.bbc.co.uk/keyskills/extra/module1/1.shtml

**IEP or Individual Education Plan.** The IEP is a planning, teaching and reviewing tool. It records key short-term targets and strategies for an individual pupil that are different from or additional to those in place for the rest of the group or class. Pupils with learning difficulties should ALL have an IEP, and gifted and talented students given ones too.

**KS or Key Stage.** A child's progress through school is marked out in Key Stages. Each Key Stage covers a number of school years and there is a test at the end of each Key Stage, starting at Key Stage 1 and finishing at Key Stage 4.

**Key Stage tests.** These are sometimes named SATs (Standard Attainment Tests). At the end of each Key Stage pupils must take tests (KS 1 and 2) or be assessed by their teacher (KS1 and 3) to see how well they have done.

**Key Stage 1 teacher assessments, tasks and tests.** Teacher assessment for seven-year-olds covers: reading, writing, speaking and listening, maths, science. These assessments take account of how your child performed in Key Stage 1 tasks and tests for seven-year-olds. The tasks and tests can be taken at a time the school chooses. They last for less than three hours altogether. The results are not reported separately but are used to help the teacher assess your child's work. By the age of seven, most children are expected to achieve level 2. The teacher assessment is moderated by your Local Authority. This is to make sure teachers make consistent assessments of children's work.

**Key Stage 2 tests and teacher assessments**. Key Stage 2 tests for 11-year-olds cover: English – reading, writing (including handwriting) and spelling, maths – including mental arithmetic, science. These tests are taken on set days in mid-May, and last less than five-and-a-half hours altogether. The teacher assessment covers: English, maths, science. By the age of 11, most children are expected to achieve level 4.

**Key Stage 3 teacher assessments.** The Key Stage 3 teacher assessment for 14-year-olds covers: English, maths, science, history, geography, modern foreign languages, design and technology, Information and Communication Technology (ICT), art and design, music, physical education, citizenship, religious education. By the age of 14, most children are expected to achieve level 6.

**Key Stage test scores.** No child can "fail" a test but they are expected to attain certain levels. Within each level there are subsections: a = top of the level, b = middle of the level, and c = bottom of the level. Children are expected to move up at least two levels every year, so if your child is marked at seven as being a 2c in English, by the time he is eight he should be a 2a, by the time he is nine he should be a 3b, at ten he should be a 4a and so on. TOP TIP: The best website I found to explain this in detail is not a government website but a primary school one. It is not a hugely professional site but it does the job better than anyone else! http://www.woodlands-junior.kent.sch.

| Key Stage | Age range and School Years | Minimum Level expected in Key Stage tests |
|---|---|---|
| Key Stage 1 | 5-7 year olds (Years 1-3) | Level 2 |
| Key Stage 2 | 8-11 year olds (Years 4-6) | Level 4 |
| Key Stage 3 | 12-14 year olds (Years 7-9) | Level 6 |
| Key Stage 4 | 15-16 year olds (Years 10-11) | Grade C or above in GCSE, Pass at GNVQ |
| Key Stage 5 | 17-18 year olds (Years 12-13) | E grade or above at A Level |

**Kumon Schools.** Kumon offer individualised after-school study programmes designed to help children of all ages and abilities to fulfil their potential in maths and English. Children work at their own pace, starting at an easy level and then progressing only after they have got an exercise entirely right. This method, developed originally in Japan, can really help children who are struggling with maths and English at school; it is soothing, repetitive and exhaustive in covering the basics. But every child is different and some may benefit from its approach: http://www.kumon.co.uk/

**LAC.** Looked-After Children.

**LA or LEA.** Local Authority or Local Education Authority. The term 'local education authority' (or LEA) or Local Authority (LA) describes a type of council which has responsibility for providing education to pupils of school age in its area. Their overall education remit covers all the ages in their area from early years to adult education. Most crucially, it should be sufficiently organised so that there are enough places at good schools for all the pupils in the area. Whether it does this or not is another matter. TOP TIP: Most LAs have parent helplines: if they do, use the helpline or advisors but remember their advice will always be biased. The LA may well want your child to attend a failing school because they wish the places in the school to be filled, you may well have different ideas.

**Learning styles.** There are four different learning styles: visual, auditory, kinaesthetic, and tactile (touching). Children learn in different ways and may benefit from being stimulated to learn by one style above another. So for example, if they are "kinaesthetic" in their learning style, they may learn better by doing drama and PE. Every child is entitled to have a "personalised" learning scheme which caters specifically to their preferred learning style. Most schools haven't got their head around this at all.

**LSA.** Learning Support Assistant. LSAs are not fully qualified teachers and usually support children with learning difficulties.

**MLD.** Mild Learning Difficulty.

**National Curriculum.** All state schools must teach the content laid out in the National Curriculum: http://curriculum.qca.org.uk/

**National Curriculum Levels.** All pupils undergo national tests and teacher assessments at ages 7, 11 and 14. The school then must send a report to parents telling them what National Curriculum Levels their child has reached in both tests and teacher assessments. During Key Stages 1-3, progress in most National Curriculum subjects is assessed against eight levels. At the end of Key Stages 1, 2 and 3 the school will send you a report telling you what level your child is working at. At Key Stage 1 the level will be based on the teacher's assessment, taking into account your child's performance in several tasks and tests. At Key Stage 2 the level will reflect the teacher's assessment and your child's national test results. At Key Stage 3 the level will be based on the teacher's assessment. TOP TIP: Check to see if your child is achieving at the expected levels or above: http://www.direct.gov.uk/en/Parents/Schoolslearninganddevelopment/ExamsTestsAndTheCurriculum/DG_4016665

**NUT.** National Union of Teachers. The biggest and most powerful teaching union. TOP TIP: Sometimes the NUT can assist parents if they have a grievance.

**OFSTED.** Office for Standards in Education. The school inspectorate. Their reports on schools aim to say what a school is good at and what they need to improve upon. Their website is excellent and very easy to use. Their reports should be read before deciding upon any state school. TOP TIP: Look at the overall judgements upon a school and the school's targets.

Remember that these reports can be off-the-mark though: http://www.ofsted.gov.uk

**PANDA.** Performance and Assessment Reports. Produced by the Office For Standards in Education (Ofsted) and issued every year to schools. These reports compare the results of a particular school with schools in similar areas and see whether the school is doing better or worse than them. They make for very interesting reading but can be unreliable indicators about how good a school is. TOP TIP: Look at your school's PANDA scores on their Ofsted report; if there is a definite pattern of under-achievement, you need to start addressing your concerns to the headteacher.

**Parent Partnership Service.** Nearly all LEAs have parent partnership services whereby the LEA will provide an advisor for parents to guide them through the SEN process if it is required. TOP TIP: Contact your LEA for more information.

**PEP.** Personal Education Plan. TOP TIP: Every child is entitled to one of these if they are not achieving their potential.

**PMLD.** Profound and Multiple Learning Difficulties. TOP TIP: Ask for an assessment as soon as possible if you believe your child has PMLD.

**PTA.** Parent Teacher Association. TOP TIP: Get involved with the PTA; you'll get to know your child's school better that way and will be helping out too.

**Performance Tables or League Tables.** The Department for Education and Skills publishes comparative secondary and 16-18 performance tables each year. The tables report achievements in public examinations and vocational qualifications in secondary schools and Further Education sector colleges. Primary school performance tables are published by local education authorities and report the achievements of pupils at the end of Key Stage 2. TOP TIP: Remember that many schools do "vocational" subjects to boost their exam results so the league tables need to be treated with caution. The key scores to look for are the achievements in English, Maths and Science.

**QCA.** The Qualifications and Curriculum Authority. This the government quango which monitors all the qualifications in the country, issuing the relevant criteria for exams to the exam boards. They are a very powerful body indeed, and have a huge influence over the lives of pupils and teachers in the land. They are unfortunately frequently wrong-headed in their judgements and unaccountable for their actions. Perhaps most disastrously, they have effectively encouraged mass cheating for over a decade now by refusing to abolish coursework. TOP TIP: Check out their website, which is stuffed full of resources and information for parents, pupils and teachers: http://www.qca.org.uk

**SENCO.** Special Educational Needs Co-ordinator. TOP TIP: Get to know your school's SENCO if you feel your child is struggling with the work. Ask for an assessment.

**School Action.** When a class or subject teacher identifies that a pupil has special educational needs they provide interventions that are additional to or different from those provided as part of the normal curriculum. An IEP will usually be devised. TOP TIP: Try and be involved as much as you can in this process: you will need to help out if your child is to catch up.

**School Action Plus.** If School Action fails, a pupil moves onto School Action Plus. The targets should be different from or additional to School Action. A new IEP should be devised. TOP TIP: Make sure that your child is receiving something above and beyond what most pupils receive in class if they are on School Action Plus.

**School Profile:** a school's annual report. TOP TIP: Log onto http://schoolsfinder.direct.gov.uk/ and type in the name of the relevant school to find out what your school has to say about itself. Remember that schools always accentuate the positive. What you need to look at is their targets: these are their weaknesses.

**SEN.** Special Educational Needs. If a pupil has a learning difficulty then he will be dubbed as having "special educational needs". It is vital you and your child are NOT ashamed of this. TOP TIP: Remember to ask for a proper assessment of your child if you have any doubts about their ability to keep up with the work they are set. If the school's assessment is not satisfactory, ask for an educational psychologist to assess your child.

**SLD.** Severe Learning Difficulties. TOP TIP: If your child has SLD, make sure you apply for a Statement of Special Educational Needs as soon as possible (see below).

**Special Schools.** State schools in England and Wales which are provided by local education authorities for certain children with special educational needs. TOP TIP: Many of these schools are closing, but some have been saved when parents have protested about their closure. Often, these schools have staff who specialise in teaching pupils with severe learning difficulties.

**Specialist Schools.** Don't confuse these with Special Schools.

They are very, very different! This type of school includes technology, languages, sports and art colleges operating in England. TOP TIP: Specialist schools can select 10% of their pupils in the subject the school specialises in. Since many schools specialise in music or sports, this effectively means that pupils who have received extra tuition in the subject or subjects that the school specialises in have the edge when applying.

**Statements of Special Educational Needs.** If School Action and School Action Plus (see Special Needs section) fail to solve a pupils' learning difficulties then he will be assessed again by the school and LEA and may be given a Statement of Special Educational Needs. Only 3% of pupils receive such a statement. The statement is a legally binding document and is reviewed every year. TOP TIP: If you feel that your child has a learning difficulty, be pushy about having your child assessed for SEN because it can mean extra resources, attention and teaching for your child.

**UCAS.** Universities and Colleges Admissions Service — central agency for processing applications for undergraduate courses. It may well be worth checking the UCAS website before making final decisions on A Levels as the website will inform you about what A Levels are necessary for specific degree courses. TOP TIP: Most of the top universities will expect pupils to have A*-C grade GCSEs in the respected academic subjects: English, English Literature, Maths, a Humanities subject such as History or Geography, a Modern Foreign Language such as French and Latin, and Science. Nearly all medical courses will expect pupils to have "triple" or "double" Science GCSE: http://www.ucas.com